COPYRIGHT PAGE

Copyright 2018 – John McGuigan

DEDICATIONS

To Helen, for everything, everything.

Standing on the shoulders of giants. To all the fantastic people I have learned from.

And Dr Susan Friedman, my knowledge wouldn't be where it is if it were not for you.

TABLE OF CONTENTS

ABOUT THE AUTHOR

If your dogs are pulling and being aggressive, I can help you to transform them into well behaved and obedient dogs in only fifteen minutes a day.

Does your dog pull on the lead when you take it for a walk, and you end up tugging like a maniac? Do you find your dog being aggressive towards other dogs? Maybe they bark inappropriately and you get embarrassed. Some dogs are continually jumping up on people, or they don't come to you when you call them. Does any of this sound familiar?

•   Perhaps you think you can't afford dog training. In one hour I can show you things that will make a difference in your dog forever.

•   Maybe you believe that it takes too long and you don't have the time. All you need is fifteen minutes a day and I can help you find those fifteen minutes. You'll be surprised.

•   Some people think that positive reinforcement training doesn't work. Let me ask you a question: do you work for a living? Do you get paid to do a job? I'm not trying to be smart here, but that's positive reinforcement.

 I know it's not easy juggling work, family and trying to keep your dog happy… especially frustrating when you're already familiar with positive dog training techniques but you've got very little time to apply it. It's always "one day" and something that you promise yourself you'll get around to eventually.

 So I just want to take a minute to let you know that it can be done. How can I say this with any confidence? Because I know how you feel. Getting quality time with my animals wasn't easy for me either and I certainly had challenges of my own just like you do now.

If I knew then what I know now, my dogs would have been glorious…

 See, I'd dabbled with psychology, read all the self-improvement books and philosophy – I'm sure you have too. I have a science degree, so Pavlovian Conditioning resonated with me. From what I could tell it basically fell into two different camps – the nurturing parent model that you'd use with kids, or the strict father model that you were supposed to use on your dog.

 I started training my own dogs about ten years ago. At the time we had Superstar Mollie, who was a tricoloured border collie cross. She was a little highly strung but sharp as a tack when it came to training. Bosco, my boy, came to us in January 2001 at eight weeks old. He was a Dogue de Bordeaux, the most handsome example of the breed I have ever seen (although, admittedly, I am a little biased). Not too tall and built like a tank, he loved a ball, tug games and treats but unfortunately I learnt compulsion training as my start and we didn't have an awful lot of fun during the first few years of his life.

 I'd been taught wrongly that he was being dominant and that I had to control him through rank reduction programmes and the like. Macho dominance - be the big man, like testosterone-filled guys in a gym. I bet you know what I'm talking about. I was too heavy handed with my dog, so I was referred to a dog trainer… reluctantly.

A year later, I got our sweet, sweet girl Kitty, the Neapolitan Mastiff. A great example of the breed, tight skin on her body and only a little loose skin and she could move like a greyhound.

Being a cross over trainer, I have the benefit of experience of both camps. I now use no physically aversive techniques and only occasionally use some techniques which may be mildly aversive psychologically. I can categorically state that aversive techniques do work in training and can have a short term effect on the manifestations of some problem behaviours. Do I agree with them anymore? Absolutely not.

Outdated aversive methods from World War Two just made my dog more aggressive towards other dogs.

I have had a few discussions both online and at conferences on the use of aversive training and am also very careful and deliberate to state that I no longer use nor agree with punitive training. Having said that, when I started training all those years ago I successfully taught all my dogs to walk on a loose leash, recalls and down-stays using a prong collar.

Skinner proved all those moons ago that positive punishment does work. I am not proud of using these techniques in the past but I am where I am today, in part, because of them and my knowledge of them, although my relationship with my three very special dogs unfortunately suffered as a result and due to the early death of Bosco, I didn't get the opportunity to fully repair that. But I hope I did go some way towards it.

Which brings me to the way I train now. Basically I started to read everything I could. The Real Dog Whisperer Paul Owens. Ian Dunbar has played a massive roll in my learning, along with Stanley Coren, Jean Donaldson, Sophia Yin, Ray Coppinger and many others. I started to apply the science, and the science worked. The shift for me was from obedience to partnership and participation.

As I got better at training, friends, family and work mates would ask for advice and my girlfriend encouraged me to start my own business and make it a bit more official. I loved the appeal of different learning styles, so dog training became an outlet for my passion. Now I take on most cases from recall and general manners to separation distress and aggression cases. Most of my experience comes from dealing with dog-dog aggression as I have suffered through it myself.

For me it's all about compassion and the welfare of the animals that don't speak our language. The most I now give to a dog is a verbal non reward marker and rely heavily on counter conditioning through positive reinforcement and am using Grisha Stewart's Behavioural Adjustment Training which allows the dog much more control and choice in their environment.

If you'd like some feedback on your on situation then you can contact me via

www.GlasgowDogTrainer.co.uk
Facebook Glasgow Dog Trainer & Behaviour Consultant

CHAPTER ONE – YOUR DOG IS JUMPING UP ON PEOPLE

Every day I help dog owners whose dogs are pulling and being aggressive to transform them into well-behaved, obedient dogs in only 15 minutes a day. Is that a big claim?

If you put the work in, yep, that's accurate.

Now I've been working with dogs for quite some time and initially got involved because I was taught incorrectly how to work with my own dog. So in order to bring you up-to-date and let you know who I am. I got my own dog, my first dog, in 2000 or 1999, and then I got a puppy a couple of years after that, and I was shown really old-school training methods, using choke chains and dominance-based training. I ended up really wrecking my dogs, both of them, through those methods, and then I was put onto a more progressive approach to training, and that was probably about 10 years ago.

After I started going down that path, I just started learning more about it, reading books, attending seminars, watching DVDs. It just picked up from there, and gave advice to people, and then they were asking to pay me. Then it was friends of friends, and then their friends, and so on. I've been doing it professionally about eight years now, and two years ago I went through the jump to do it full-time, and I haven't looked back. Now I've got something like 14,000 followers on Facebook right now. I've got, I was going to say rabid but that's the wrong word to use, but I've got a fanatically loyal fan base. Honestly my clients love what I do, they follow what I do, they listen to my advice, and if they apply what I teach them, it just works.

It will work if you do it, and if it's not working there's always a reason for it.

See I'm a behaviour consultant as well as a dog trainer, I like those two separate terms. So why is my approach different to just a bog standard, dog training guy that I can hire down the street?

The first thing is my commitment to CPD. I attend multiple seminars every year. I watch DVD seminars. I read books, I keep up-to-date with people. I keep myself up-to-date with the latest training, which is coming from research universities into learning so this is not coming from somebody who's got an opinion on dog training or a guy off the television. It's coming from people who are studying this as a full-time research position, the same way as we would study physics or medicine.

We are absolutely committed to that, and lots of dog training clubs have not updated their methods for 15 years. I say to people, "If you went to your doctor, and your doctor hadn't done any CPD in 15 years, you'd be running out the door." So just because we've always got results, doesn't mean it's the best way to do it, and I differ, or we differ, because we try and apply the most up-to-date, scientific knowledge to clients with their dogs in a way that's easy to understand. It's fast, effective, and it's kind, which if it's done properly, with the minimal amount of behavioural fallout to the dog.

So in this first chapter we're especially looking at one particular problem, which is the dog jumping up on you, or jumping up on other people. Now I've already prepared three short videos for you and I'll give a little bit of background as to why dogs jump. They learn it as puppies most often, and most puppies are cute. People greet puppies by approaching them head on, and putting their hands out. The puppy jumps up on top of them, and then they get petted, so the puppy learns from an early age that they receive some sort of physical or verbal contact from strangers by jumping on them.

What happens then is the puppy then grows older, and what was cute in a 12-week-old, or an eight-week-old Labrador is now not cute, and a nine-month-old Labrador that's been running through a muddy puddle, and you're wearing your spanking new chinos that are just out of the washing machine. So that's where it comes from. What happens then is that people start either using corrective training, so they'll tell the dog, "No," or they'll pull the dog back on the lead, or they ask the dog to sit when he can't sit because he's too aroused.

It then just becomes this big cycle that, actually, our attention to the dog by telling him to sit, by shouting at him, by pushing him away, that ends up reinforcing the behaviour, the same way as a child who's not given enough attention, their behaviour of being destructive, annoying, rude, or whatever label you want to put on it, becomes reinforced by the parents interacting with them. So that's where problem of jumping generally comes from.

Also, there's also a problem with young dogs because lots of dogs don't know where their own bodies are, so they don't realize it when they jump up to your face that their feet leave the ground, and by teaching a dog body awareness about where his front feet and his back feet are, we very often make massive in-roads into jumping, by just teaching a dog where his feet are.

So that is, proprioception is the word, proprioception. Sensory awareness.

So this first video's only about 20 seconds long or something like that. So this is an old friend of mine, Angela.

https://www.youtube.com/watch?v=5zR3FEBDwOQ

That dog's seven-month-old Alfie. So you see here as soon as I walk in he start jumping on me. I know, I see you jumping on me. So Alfie's seven months old and his mum is my old schoolmate, so I haven't seen Angela in 20-something years and nearly 30 actually, and she called me and asked me for some help with Alfie. So what's happened here is Alfie is looking to say hello by jumping, so that's what he's looking for. He's looking to access some sort of reinforcement from me, and he's learnt that the vehicle to do that is jumping.

Okay, the next clip that you see, Angela has him on a lead, and the only mistake that we make here is I've not said to her to hold him away him from me just now. Okay, she's on a lead, and as a first start with her, we're managing the behaviour, or I'm sorry, we're managing the environment so the unwanted behaviour of jumping doesn't happen. We could watch that one.

https://www.youtube.com/watch?v=8MNf8S0kPJY&feature=youtu.be

This is just a few minutes later. Look for the sit up. So every time that he sits or puts four feet on the ground, I click and put a treat away from me. It doesn't matter how much he's doing it. He doesn't need to sit, or he just needs to have four feet on the ground. That a boy. I'll give him a treat.

And he gets a click and a treat again. Lovely. You see how each time I throw the treat away so that I'm not actually inviting him into my space? Excellent. Okay, cool.

Now you might be wondering how much time was there between the first and second video?

Well, they were back-to-back. We had done one previous training session with Alfie. It was on the Friday night, and I think I'd been up on either the Wednesday or the Thursday afternoon, and had done one hour training session with Alfie before then, which had done about half an hour of teaching him that the click means a treat is going to happen. So every time he has his feet on the ground, I'll click and put a treat down.

I'm conditioning the dog - his behaviour causes me to click the button, and when I click the button I'll give him a treat.

Now you might think that the reason for pushing the treat further and further away, is to get him more freedom of movement, or to make him feel safe. With him, he's super friendly, anyway, but what I'm actually wanting to do is if I put the treat away, and he eats that treat, he's now further away from me than he was, which means he's less likely to jump on me the next time, because he's now six feet away from me. If he's now six feet away from me, I can now click and treat him being six feet away from me.

The actual proximity to you or to the person is part of the issue, because you're right there, and therefore you're jumpable. You're able to be touched. So even with, you'll see in the next clip, we'll put that on in a second, but even with him being off-lead, if we keep doing this, if I click and treat him being four feet away from me, and keep him there by putting a treat four feet or more away from me, he now has got no reason to approach me, because he's just saying that, "This is the easiest game in the world. I just sit back four feet away from you and you throw treats at me." All right, this is just the start of it.

This is the first session that we've done with this. Once we've broken the habit of the dog jumping, we can now ask him to go into his bed, or to retrieve a toy for us whenever we come through the door. Now with nice, clean training, which is not that difficult, within the space of about half an hour we have started to teach Alfie to keep away from us when we come through the door.

He now has another option other than jumping on us. He can now sit back from us. The questions I ask, and for anybody that's watching this who has a dog that has a problem jumping, how many times when your dog has jumped, have you had to deal with your dog jumping? So you're already investing time and effort all the time trying to either manage or stop problem jumping, and if we take some of that time, and with a little bit of planning and a little bit of thoughtfulness, then we can get in before the problem behaviour starts, and reinforce an alternative behaviour.

Actually, that's the crux of what we want to do. I try and teach, rather than just saying the barking is a problem or the jumping is a problem, or the chewing my slippers is a problem, what I would do is I would provide the dog with another outlet in order to achieve a similar outcome.

Now you would imagine the earlier you can catch the dog, the younger the dog is, the better ... What if the dog's seven years old? If your dog's seven years old, you just need to do more work, and what I would always say there is if we use the analogy of you've been driving for seven years, and tomorrow I now change the order of the foot pedals. That's now going to be difficult for you to rewire your body, because you've already had so much practice practicing the previous clutch, brake, accelerator, if we now rearrange those so it's accelerator, brake, clutch, or some other permutation of that.

So what you want to do then is we can use other things, like we can use baby gates or the lead in order to prevent the dog from doing the unwanted behaviour, which is access to me. So we can use a physical barrier to prevent that, and then continue to do this. It's called the matching law, which is basically, and it's a scientific law. Its laws of learning, that a behaviour which has been reinforced 90% in that scenario will happen 90% of the time, and we're having to address that balance so that the wanted behaviour now has the greater percentages.

Okay. Once the dog learns that it's supposed to keep its feet on the ground and keep distance with you, is that then transferrable to the next person that comes to the door, or the next member of the household?

What you want to do is you want to get the dog practiced and doing it with everybody, so if it only happens with one person, he will only do that with one person. So the rule is you really want him to do it in roundabout with a dozen different people in a dozen different situations, so that the dog starts to discern, "Oh, right, it's everybody that I greet like this."

One of the other ways that one of our colleagues teaches it is this behaviour from humans towards young dogs, of my hands approaching you, that's now the signal to sit rather than jump up. What will happen is now when you're doing this properly is you moving towards the puppy with your hands outstretched, the dog will now sit down and wait until we pet them. That can be done in a very similar way to what we've just done there.

So how long would it take you, if you were walking away from this book tonight, and applying this to your doggy now, how long do you think it would take for you to see a measurable difference?

If you did this properly, you would see a result, doing it properly, within 10 minutes easily. If you go back in tomorrow, if you go in tomorrow, you have to then do it again. So it's things like being prepared to walk through the door already armed with your treats or whatever, or if your guests are coming in, be ready to have your dog on a lead and be ready for that so that we're not firefighting. We're actually, what I always think with problem behaviours is what we do is we fit smoke detectors. We don't put out fires.

It's prevention, not cure.

So let me talk you through the exact sequence then. Is it clicker first, then they respond by sitting down or putting their feet on the ground, then they get the treat?

So it's called SMART training, see, mark, and reinforce training. Okay? SMART. So you see the behaviour you like, you mark it with the clicker or with a word, good or yes, and then you reinforce it, and if you get that sequence well enough, if you observe the behaviour that you like, you mark it, and you reinforce it, that's the behaviour that's now more likely to happen.

The treat is the reinforcement. Some dogs don't like treats, so what you could use is you'd use a toy. What I do with my dog is, I've had my new dog since December, and the first thing that I do when I go through the door is I get down on my knees and give him access to me while I say hello to him. So what he wants to do is he wants access to my face to jump up and say hi, and what I do is I get down and say to him, "I'll give you that access and I'll say hi to you."

I'm giving him what he wants, but he starts learning that this, me saying hello to him, only happens when he's got four feet on the ground, and it took a few weeks of doing that, and now what happens is I can walk through the door, walk into the kitchen, unpack my staff, so put my car keys down, and take my jacket off, and then I can say hello to him, but I started by getting a little bit of what I wanted, and then gradually getting the whole picture. It doesn't take long if you're consistent.

You're actually getting down to his level.

The only reason he's trying to come up is because that's the level you're at, and he's trying to come to you, so if you go to him ... It's like talking to a small child. I was always taught to kneel down and look them in the eye. Instead of looming over this poor little guy who's looking up at a giant and it's the same thing. I like that. I like that a lot.

So the third video is basically very similar to the second one, but Alfie's off-leash.

Its moments later. It's, honestly, I've gone back out the door, paused for 30 seconds, and rang the doorbell again.

Now that rustling is me preparing the treats. So that's he jumps once, and a click, got four feet on the ground, and straightaway he's ... Because he's already practiced this.

Okay. Now that is really basic. What we can do is we can teach him that the doorbell ringing is a signal for him to go to his bed, and then we reinforce him in his bed, but this is just to break the back of the problem behaviour. It's just we need to get him somewhere and start reinforcing something that we like, and then we can build on that.

So when I'm teaching ... I think it's almost as much human teaching as it is dog teaching. Almost as much.

But there are some typical hiccups or gaffes that I see the human making at this point. So I've taught them this, I've taken them through this process, I've taught them the acronym, I've got them chucking treats. Where does it fall down? What can go wrong?

The stuff that I've learned, one of my great mentors who I've learned from Dr. Susan Friedman, she's always been on about antecedent arrangement, so that's the preparation of your environment or setting yourself up for success.

So an analogy that you would use for that is if you find it difficult to get out of bed in the morning to go to the gym at 6:30, pack your bag, prepare your protein shake, get everything ready, so the only thing you need to do is get out of bed, and put your shoes on, and get out the door. So that's setting yourself up for success. Okay?

So what I do is we'll talk about how to fade the treats in a minute, because that's often a concern that the clients have, but I have a tin of treats at the door. I've got a little balcony out here, which is that way, and I've got a tin of treats at the balcony door, and I've got a tin of treats on my unit across here, which means that if the balcony door is open of an evening, and I hear people outside, I can go outside and immediately start reinforcing quiet behaviour from him.

Where clients, where they fall down is they don't prepare adequately for this, for guests coming in. If you know your guests are coming in, generally people know beforehand that they're going to get a visitor who's going to come out to the house, so we could have a lead at the door, plus treats, and the doorbell goes, we clip the dog on a lead. We hold the dog back as we open the door, and we now start clicking and treating the behaviours that we want.

Over time, we'll have to use the lead less and less, because that's the behaviour that the dog does in that situation. If your dog jumps on you when you come in the house, then I would have your treat bag which you keep in the car, and as you leave your car you pick up the treat bag. Okay?

And you're setting that up, and actually not being surprised that your dog jumps, because I'll say to people when I'm go in and see them, "How many times has your dog jumped on you?" They'll say, "He's jumped on me every time I've come in the door for the last two years." I say, "So we know he's going to do that, don't we?" So if we know he's going to do it, we can do something about it, so setting yourself up for success beforehand, and that certainly helps.

How we get rid of the food is that you now use praise as reinforcement for the dog. Once the dog's got in that habit of settling down, or going to his mat, or going to his bedroom when we come through the door, we walk in the door and we say to him, "That's a good lad. Well done, son. That's really nice."

Then we can go and say hello to him there, because really what he wants to do is he wants to say hello to us. The food is just helping us get the behaviour that we want. So you're still reinforcing the behaviour of settled behaviour in his bed, but you're using praise to reinforce it now rather than food.

Okay. So if someone was struggling to have control over their dog, or the way they see it as control of the dog, the dog's jumping up and down, they can basically run this process now based on what they're seeing right here.

Regarding the clicker, could they snap their fingers? Could they do something different, whistle?

Yep, the easiest one is just to use a marker word. One of my clients, he uses "Boom", and actually he'll say, every time the dog does something, he says, "Boom," and gives the dog a treat. You can click your tongue to get the dog's attention.

I would generally use a clean word that you're only going to use in this instance. You know, so a "Nice" and "good," and then you give him his treat, but if you're using a marker word, you always have to follow that up with a treat, the same as you do with a clicker.

But this is just to teach the dog. The clicker or the marker word is a teaching tool, and once the dog knows how to do it, you don't need to teach them. You just need to keep reinforcing it in order to keep that behaviour strong, but you could use a word. What's really cool about this as well, is that even if we get it wrong at the start, what we end up doing is giving the dog a couple extra treats. That's the worst that happens. The dog gets a couple of freebies.

He's not getting shocked! Or spiked in the neck. Pushing him away, correcting him on his collar, we're not doing any of these things. The worst thing that happens is we give one extra couple of treats. It's really cool. It's very humane. It's very respectful.

Clients love the fact that in the space of 20 minutes, you've basically supplied a step-by-step recipe to solve a problem that a lot of people have. It's practical, it's useful, and it's fast, efficient. I'm not joking about 15 minutes a day. This doesn't need to take a lot. It's not hard. You can do it on the breaks in the middle of Coronation Street. It's not that difficult.

It's just it works if you do it. It works if you work it.

I think the biggest criticism of this style of training is that it's not as fast as punitive training, or if you're using corrections, for want of a more diplomatic way to talk about it, but the science, the experiments don't back that thesis up, or that hypothesis up.

It's just that we are, as a society, we are so much more skilled at stopping unwanted behaviour, telling people, "No, stop doing that," and we're actually not that skilled at reinforcing behaviours that we want. So it's not quicker. It's just if we understand what the animal or what the person is looking to achieve by their behaviour, we can provide that through a different behaviour.

When I teach this in a live format, like in a workshop or a seminar kind of format, the biggest thing is that people go, "I can actually do this. It's nice and clean. It's easy, and I don't have to give him, my dog a hard time to do it." It takes the pressure off of both them and the dog, and they can now actually start liking their dog again, because it's not that they don't like the dog, it's that they don't like the behaviours that the dog is doing, and that then affects how they see the dog.

That's what people tell me, is that they see this very often, "Oh, my dog's actually really cool." "Yeah, your dog's really cool. He just needs help getting there." That's the nicest thing for me, and that's what people tend to give me feedback about, is that they can actually start liking the dog again.

I always remember hearing about working with children, it was always criticize the behaviour, don't criticize the identity. It's not that they're a bad kid. It's a good kid with a bad behaviour, or a not useful behaviour. And that behaviour only happens under certain circumstances, and that behaviour is looking to access an outcome, and by looking at those two things, we can then change that behaviour.

So my aim with this book is to cover a number of these with different topics that we know are common, frequent issues that bug dog owners. If you wanted to get in touch with me at the moment, the easiest way is through my website, which is www.glasgowdogtrainer.co.uk, or you can email me directly at info@glasgowdogtrainer.co.uk, or via Facebook, which is Glasgow Dog Trainer and Behaviour Consultant, but the email is the easiest way to get in touch with me.

Please remember I'm a very busy man. I'm working with a lot of people. I do around about 20 appointments a week.

Bruce and Gillian, I also give them, between the two of them they probably get maybe another 20 or so appointments on top of that every few weeks. I usually get booked about 10 days to two weeks in advance.

At the end of the day the bottom line is that people end up with a better relationship with their dog, that they perceive as now being well-behaved and in control, that actually the dog's getting his needs met, and you're respecting the dog, and communicating to the animal the way it needs to be communicated with.

The dog's getting needs met in a way that meets our needs.

Don't just train your dog. Just get out there, train your dog and enjoy it.

CHAPTER TWO - YOUR DOG IS PULLING ON THE LEAD

In this chapter I want to give you more information that you can apply today, and it will work today. If you're interested in having an obedient doggy who's having a good life as a warm, loving companion to you and is not just a prop on the end of a rope to demonstrate as a trophy. This is all about a win/win relationship between the human and the animal.

In this chapter we're going to look at loose lead walking, with the dog NOT pulling on the lead – the dog walking with you, whatever you want to call that and we're looking to teach the dog and the owner to walk together without the owner being pulled. Now this is a really common problem for a variety of reasons which we'll talk about as the chapter goes on, and it can be a difficult thing to resolve unless we do the right things. It's quite a big topic so there's a lot to talk about and I've got a number of videos lined up to demonstrate various aspects of this problem just to make it easier for you to get your head around.

https://youtu.be/VbzYdNa0UVs

So if you click the link on this first video, this will seem a little bit out of left field. This is my friend Sam who is an acrobat and we shot this video to illustrate the difficulty that we have when we have two beings with different physical abilities trying to negotiate the same course while attached to each other. So Sam is about 22 or 23 years old and I'm 44. Sam is a professional acrobat and circus performer, so you'll see how easy it is for him to move around and how difficult it is for me to follow the same course – while attached to him.

At first you see us moving around – Sam's movement are fluid, mine are not. In fact I'm moving about like an old man. Now we come to a nice bit where we see how easy it is for Sam to get over that railing while it's so difficult for me to balance while attached to him. Then it gets really interesting when Sam goes through the railings one way and I HAVE to go through another way… because he's holding "my other side" if you like.

So this is purely to illustrate the difficulty that lots of people have with their dog. You see me having difficulty trying to get over this railing while holding onto him. So the equivalent would be like us going up a flight of stairs with your dog on the end of a lead, or going down a flight of stairs and the dog moving at a different pace from us. The dog is lower to the ground and we're higher up – depending on the height of the dog.

What I'm going to do is refer you back to this and the difficulty I had moving with Sam going through this. What we're really doing is moving around and going over, under and through a railing. It's really just two beings with different physical abilities trying to navigate the same set of obstacles. And you'll see that ultimately I go under it in a completely different way from the way that Sam does.

Sam had put on a little "Introduction To Parkour" course last year and I went along and met him. I think that one of my strengths as a teacher is trying to see things differently in order to illustrate a point. This amply demonstrates that it can be more difficult than it looks and using a novel way like that which will stick in people's minds. I'd seen Sam do a little bit of work and I though "Ah OK I can see how I can relate that to working with your dog."

I hope this video really rams home the point here – two different species linked together by a bit of metal, or cord or whatever and one of them trying to dominate the other, or not even dominating necessarily – perhaps being permissive. Now imagine how tricky that would be if I couldn't physically move like that, but he was still physically making me move like that. What he'd now have to do is DRAG me around that obstacle… and that was in a relatively low distraction environment. There's not much else going on in that setting, I can concentrate fully on what I'm doing. There's no danger, there's nothing else that's interesting, but in the real world you're going to have all these other distractions when you're out walking your dog.

Hopefully if you're a dog owner, then I've taught you a MASSIVE lesson by letting you see that video.

Okay so what often happens with loose lead walking is that the dog is pulling on the end of the lead for a variety of reasons we are not working harmoniously with our dog, the dog has different sets of interest from us and then what happens is that we use some kind of some kind of mechanical device whether that's a collar that restricts the dog or causes it some discomfort, some kind of harness which also restricts the dogs movements and all these things make it easier for us and make it more difficult for the dog to move. You get leads that have bungee cords in them which acts like a shock absorber which means we are not feeling that strain at the end of the lead, but the dog is feeling that all of the time.

Basically if you look at any piece of equipment which is designed to stop the dog from pulling it generally does that through discomfort and that discomfort might be mild but they are usually there to make it uncomfortable enough for the dog.

So in order to relieve that pulling sensation it makes the dog walk beside you and I do as much as I can to get away from that and instead teach the owner and the dog to walk together as part of a team

This brings new meaning to the phrase taking the dog for a walk – you're actually going for a walk together

https://youtu.be/zeyURdzOfxc

This is us going for a walk together and he's on a 6 foot long lead and what happens is if he moves out towards the end of the lead I will then stop and wait for him to join me again. So you see him join me again, he turns back and looks at me. This is what's known as a sniff walk with the two of us walking together, working together and I'm guiding him safely and what he does is he stops he looks at me.

My body position is nice and relaxed, I try and keep the lead as loose as I can but as you see in the video he's a little bit concerned about the two people walking past on the path that we saw. He has a little bit of a look and then you see him getting spooked – he is spooky around smells so that's why he waits for me to follow him there. Then I just slow him down, wait till he settles and then what I'm looking to do is to let him sniff away. This is relatively early on with us practising this so I'm moving around him and through the environment as well and giving him the space that he needs to explore, then you see him pull forward and I, wait till he comes back towards me and then we start walking on again. He slows down and checked in with me, he starts to speed up so I slow down.

Then I give him a little bit of prompting telling him that I want to move over a little bit to the left. So this is quite a nice walk for him and I'm telling him that I can provide him with the stuff that he likes but its contingent on both of us doing it together. So I'm not preventing him from sniffing and I'm not telling him he can't sniff I'm just saying that if he wants to sniff something we are going to go together. I'm also watching him to see what he's interested in so if he moves forward on the end of the lead he is generally pointing or moving in the direction of something that interests him so I'll slow down and wait till he reconnects with me as he did there in the video and then we will move off.

Next you see something interesting in the video and this is just to illustrate a quick point – my son moves away to dispose of the poo bag and that's why he keeps looking to his right, while my daughter continues to shoot the video. Now I asked him a couple of times to move off there but he still said no. My son Max still isn't back yet, so then when Max returns you see him starting to walk back towards me. Now when Max rejoined the group again then he's ready to move off with us.

Now one point is that I could watch that video five times and give you a different narration each time pointing out various things that are happening – there's tons in that video and that's only 2 1/2 minutes long and I am watching him the whole time to see what it is he's interested in – thinking all the while "Is that safe for you to do that?"

He's an easily spooked dog anyway because he had a whole bunch of problems before he came to live with us and we are working through them so some of his pulling on the lead are symptoms of his old problems, it's not just him pulling on the lead for the sake of pulling on the lead. That was a really nice walk for him, nice and slow, he gets to stop and sniff and he basically meanders through the environment.

The lead handling is done with my shoulders as relaxed as possible. I'm as relaxed as I can be, my knees are soft, my hips my ankles and my elbows are soft and I'm using my weight to brace him, so if you moves forward I'll move my weight away from the direction that he is pulling in so that I'm not using my arms to pull him back.

If he has nothing to pull against them he won't pull forward – it's called opposition reflex – basically it's what happens when somebody bumps you and you don't fall over, you immediately have a reflex to keep you upright and the way that it works with dogs is that if we pull forward they'll pull against that force, so very often you see people walking down the street yanking the lead and all they are doing the whole time is giving their dog something to pull against

You will usually see people on their phone or striding up the path basically dragging the dog with them to get the walk over as quickly as possible, or the last thing we are looking at is the dog - they're looking at everything else or chatting with everyone else but the dog gets the minimum of attention. The dog is just there to be walked so right from the start in the video you can see the rapport and relationship between me and the animal which is probably lacking in a lot of people. This is work that needs to be done at the start, I'm not saying that this is what all of our walks will be like forever, but this is how a walk will be when I'm teaching a client at first how to walk with the dog. I put my phone on silent I don't listen to music and I'm watching what he's doing and I am very aware of what he's doing and because I know him, I'm glancing up at the environment.

I'm not scanning the environment all the time but I glanced at the environment to see if there is something there that he is likely to be concerned about and it means that I can then start dealing with that before it happens, or if it is something that is interesting to him so things like trains, anywhere that the scent is strong, so the edge of things lampposts, drains, all these things are interesting for your dog because scents get stuck in them. By looking and planning your walk up the path you can see as you walk what he is likely to pull towards as he gets within 6 feet of it. I know this is my job and I know this is what I do full time, but just having some awareness of your dog and that he perceives the world definitely from you. This way you end up with a more symbiotic relationship with the animal which is nice.

One of the loveliest things I've ever seen with a client and the dog was when I was sitting at traffic lights in the car and there was a man. There was a fella in his 70s with his dog - a little West Highland terrier and the two of them were more just walking together and they were just completely in sync with each other. They knew each other was there through the lead. The little dog stopped and as I watched him it wasn't that he saw the dog stopping, he felt the change in the lead position in his hand and he just slowed down and stopped, looked forward while the dog's sniffing for five or 10 seconds, and then the dog moves forward again. He felt the change in little pressure and when I say little pressure I mean it's hanging in his hand, you know, and he felt the pressure when the dog started moving on and he moved on with the dog – it's one of my favourite moments that I've ever seen with anybody with their dog – it was just really lovely because the two of them were completely in sync with each other – it was really cool.

https://youtu.be/RJZFcPJtdyE

This is a little bit of formal work that we're doing here. This is the start of me working with him so what I'm doing is I have the treats in my hand and I'm getting him to look up at the treats and when he looks up and walks with me I drop the treat down so you see I drop the treat, I walk forward, and he comes back up.

Okay so in the video you see me doing this exercise and I'm doing it for a bunch of different reasons – all of this helps him start working with you on the move and it helped teach him that sometimes we will have to walk past the things that might interest him. So just to repeat my hand is out and I have treats in it. When he catches up with me and walks with me for a set number of paces – and you see he missed my queue there – so 1234 5678 and then he gets his treat. So this is just teaching him how to work with me on the move and to concentrate because sometimes I will actually have to say "We can't stop and sniff here - in fact we need to go and you need to pay attention to me."

So if you watch that video again you'll see that I've got his attention and he'll walk with me as I start moving off. Walks with me for a few paces then you reinforce with the treat, and then again, I change direction to see if you're following me and all of this work has helped with him walking with me when I'm out. So you know this is formal training but it reaches into the informal staff. He is now getting into the habit of being with me outside, doing stuff with me and walking with me, moving with me while ignoring other things. What's interesting about this video also is this is tiring for him - because of the head position that he has to maintain. You can only do this for a little bit of time because you need to build up his fitness for it, and very often that's what the dog owner doesn't do which is build the dogs fitness up by walking with them. Owners assume the dog will just walk with them.

Now you see as we walked all the way back to the camera I'm not doing any reinforcement – he is simply walking with me now. So effectively from the point where the last treat went down the training session was over, yet he continues to walk with me so even if he had been on the lead there, you can see how one leeches into the other.

One of the first dog trainers that I trained with, Iain Dunbar said that "You don't have a dog pulling problem, you have a dog not wanting to be with you problem." The problem isn't that your dog is pulling on the lead, that's just a symptom, the actual problem is that your dog doesn't want to be with you. Your dog wants to be out elsewhere in the environment so if you work on recall and doing stuff with your dog walking all the time, the dog is more likely to want to be with you. Since I've had that dog since December and with our other dog Watson we do lots of stuff which is just doing stuff together, so that the end result is going out on a walk is just doing more stuff together, rather than I play with you with the ball in the house or in the garden, or I take you to the park and let you off the lead and then you're left to do your own thing. Whereas the more stuff you actually do with your dog the more your dog will actually want to be with you, so it's the same with any relationship – you just keeping paying into it and then the dog pays out by wanting to be with you.

You may notice that I was using a clicker in the video as well – I am marking the number of steps that I want him to walk and then reinforce it with the food. So basically asking him to hold that position trotting forward looking at me for that eight, 10, 15, 100 paces whatever we're training and then I'll mark it and reinforce it. We start low and work our way up. Hopefully its simple when I break it down like that. It's simple but it's not easy and it takes work.

Because of the approach that I take when training and especially with the people that I have learned from I'm wanting to do the least aversive of training that I possibly can, so anything I can do that gets the dog willingly working with me because I'm a source of good things or at least he's having a good experience with me, the better.

It's when you start introducing aversive tools and then all that's happening is he's working with you because he doesn't want to experience that pain or discomfort. But then that has other implications in your relationship as well. Just as in human relationships!

https://youtu.be/_AligbBg4KM

Now moving on to the next video, this is just exactly the same again but what's interesting here is that the kerb is difficult for him so he has to navigate that kerb. Now I start moving left and right here and as I approach the kerb here, as I cross it you'll see him looking around and you'll see him glancing down at that kerb. That's quite nice for him – you'll see that as he comes down off the kerb he has a little bit of a glance down to see where that is, and if the lead is too short then a lot of the time it's holding him up. So he glances as he goes over that kerb. Now he's on a long line here because he's super boisterous around people and that's just in case someone walks past, then I've got some physical control over him. The learning point here is that he's glancing down at that kerb as he's passing it. Then you see that he's getting more comfortable now and he's actually able to move across that surface now without having to look down at it.

It's kind of like you know how many steps you have in your house. If you're walking down the stairs in the dark you could count them cos you know there are thirteen steps in your stairs, and like that: he's becoming more familiar here. So that's the purpose of that and when we have the dog on too short a lead, and we're basically holding the dog's head up, so if you think about it the dog no longer has the freedom to glance down – he needs to see where he's going before he puts his feet down. I picked the kerb to give him that uneven surface and what I do when I'm training with him is I'll go across kerbs, up and down stairs as well, from pavement to grass, grass to pavement, grass to gravel, gravel to chuckies [stone chips for the non-Scots] so that he starts to register the change in surface. We see the change in colour of the texture and we can easily move from one surface to another, but the first time a dog walks on grass he thinks "What the hell is this?" And all of these things can get in the way of the dog walking next to us, because it's different for them and they move differently from us. Remember also that the dog is barefoot!

It might look like he got a wee jackpot reward at the end there, but in actuality we don't think "jackpots" improve performance, but it is certainly something nice to do for your dog. I think I just gave him whatever I had left in my hand cos it was in my hand anyway; he's as well just having it. He thinks "Oh cool I get an extra few pieces of sausage from Dad."

https://youtu.be/RGzg9FhRrTU

This next video brings in stairs. So when we're doing stair work it's the same as with everything else, we have to do moving forward and back, targeting with my hand and we have to move both left and right. Because if we're only doing one side then the dog ends up with muscular imbalances in one side. If I only get him to target on the left hand side he will naturally be looking up over his right shoulder. This side of his body is getting more work so he'll get tighter muscles on one side and not so much muscular development on the other side – so that's why you need to work both when you're doing training like this.

There's a traditional dog training thing with walking the dog on the left. That's still a really pervasive attitude across dog training. Where this came from was that historically we had our gun on the right, so the pistol or rifle would be held in the right hand so the dog was on the left. So whether that's gun dog training or military or whatever, you would have your firearm in your right hand and the dog on the left. There are still dog clubs that teach loose lead walking by having your dog always on the left. The rules I have is that as long as you're not playing merry-go-round with the lead crossing the back of your arms or stepping across it all the time, the dog is walking with you and he's not tripping you up, he's pretty much free to move harmoniously with you.

So if you're walking down the street with your wife or your husband or significant other, if they move across the street to look in a shop window you wouldn't say "No no, you have to walk on this side, I walk on that side". It's ridiculous. So when I'm doing this – if you're doing exercise like this to get your dog to walk with you, then you have to train BOTH sides.

So in this video you'll see me teaching him how to navigate stairs with me. Now what he would generally do is race down the stairs in front of him because that's easy for him. But when he's attached to me what happens is that it's not easy for me. So what I'm doing in this video is I'm walking forward with him, and I'm putting the treats down in front of him which is encouraging him to look down as well, so he's not just racing along. You'll see that he actually stops himself, because the treat bounced down the stairs. He might just want to race down the stairs because it's easier for him, but this is teaching him how to move slowly with me.

So imagine if you live in a block of flats, you're carrying your shopping and you have your dog attached to you, he needs to be able to walk slowly with you and its difficult for him. So I'm teaching him to do this on a loose lead. This is just the teaching part, and I use food for it but as he gets better he'll just learn "Oh this is what we do". You'll see that he starts to race forward and I'll stop him with the lead to tell him "That's as far as you can go."

The lead is over my shoulder here. We got back down again, this is a lot for him but he's a fit dog, he is fit for this. This is a lot of exercise to do. And it takes a lot of concentration for him to do that as well. This was in the summer where we worked on a variety of stuff with him. It's nice when you see him stop and check in with me. Now if you look at the movement in his back legs remember that, that is not a natural movement for him. Stop start, stop start. But he has to learn how to do this because that might be as fast as I can walk down the steps there. So your dog has to sometimes learn to move unnaturally for them to walk with us. Remember also that the dog is more physically able to walk then we are.

So you will see that we have an objective in mind and we go out and train and you can see the improvements in him, because when I first got him he'd never been on a lead before I got him. He literally did not know that I was on the other end of that and he would just drag me everywhere that he wanted to go. He's a big chunk of a dog, he is 32 kg of muscle – he is a total powerhouse and has a back end like a tractor. So if he wants to move me he can move me, so what I'm saying to him is he has to move with me. Yeah, cos your old man can't walk that quickly!

In the next video we see more stairs but from a different angle and we are on a different training session. You will see that he raced up in front of me and I asked him to come back. Can you wait for me? I actually guided him with my hand and then the trotting up the stairs is easy for him.

Coming down the stairs slowly is really difficult for him – the stop start, stop start it - actually takes a lot of concentration. Imagine that although he is on all four legs and he is built to be on all four legs, imagine what it will be like (and this is going back to the video with Sam at the start of this chapter). Imagine you walking down a set of stairs on all fours facing forwards, slowly, and being pulled back by the neck at the same time.

So you have all that weight moving forward on your shoulders so if your dog is not fit for that, that's difficult and what they do is they race forward so that they can get rid of that and they can balance themselves quite quickly. So there is a physical aspect to this and your dog being physically fit enough to train. To walk with us. So think that him holding himself with his back end elevated, with his hips higher up than his head and shoulders, he's got that pressure moving forward and I'm asking for him to lift his neck up at the same time, so that can be putting a lot of pressure on the dogs frame, so that's why in my treat placement I'm actually trying to put it in alignment with his spine so I'm not putting additional pressure on him on his neck.

These are all things that you need to be aware of and if you have a small dog like a Dachshund or a terrier they are looking up and they're only at your ankles anyway, so asking them to come up even further is a stretch, so you really need to look at where they're going.

So one of my dog owner friends described owning dogs for 15 years and none of the things I've pointed out in this chapter crossed his mind. He would come home from school and take the dogs out and be dragged up the street and he would be yanking them back as they barked and roared their way up the road and they did that their whole lives.

One of the exercises that I give for clients is if you can find somebody that is about 4 inches or more shorter or taller than you, start standing facing whatever direction and take 10 natural pieces forward and stop. I will then take 10 natural pieces and stop and there will be a difference in where the two of us end up, right? Because their stride or my stride will be shorter or longer than theirs. So when you are walking with someone who is shorter or taller than you – think about this – the longer strided person has to either shorten their peace or slow this straight down because the shorter person would have to walk fast to keep up. If you are familiar with the comedian Peter Kay talking about his dad running through the car park looking for the Sierra. It creates a 'walk trot walk trot' effect and you see that with people if they are walking with their child and they're walking too fast. The child will start jogging then slow down to walk then jog, jog walk, and that feels really unpleasant if you're the one that's having to change your pace, you actually can't get into a rhythm with your stride. You can't just jog or just walk - you're having to constantly change all the time. That's the same with your dog.

If you go back to the example of a small dog like a terrier, for every one stride that you take your dog might have to take six or seven strides so you have to be able to walk with them. Now what happens is that a dog's walking pace is incredibly slow. So when you saw in the video me walking with Logan across the grass that's him walking. You see in an upcoming video we are striding out and you see the dog starting to trot with us but you'll see how quickly we are walking in order to do that. You have to be aware of that as well but generally what happens is that people don't walk slow enough or don't walk fast enough, so they walk too fast for the dog to walk and too slow for the dog to trot and two things will happen there – the dog either starts pacing, which is generally both left forward and both right forward and if you were to look from above you would see their spine snaking and that's not a natural movement for a dog. Your dog should have a much more fluid movement in the spine when walking or the spine should be straight.

So if you were to look at a video of a dog sprinting, from their nose all the way back to the tail it's going in a straight line. It's the same with us. When you look at Usain Bolt – when he sprints his spine is in a straight line, it's not snaking from side to side. When we dance we move because we're moving, our feet are moving. The spine will be in a straight line so if you're getting that flexion backwards and forwards then it can cause your dog to be uncomfortable. So that's one thing that will happen – they will pace with that both left and then both right, or what they will do is pull forward to try and get the spine straight so what they'll do is just keep pulling and pulling through all that discomfort and pressure on the neck because that's actually easier for them than walking at that slower pace.

The two examples I like to give: in the UK that used to be a programme called The Cook Report and if he was interviewing a witness and they were going for a walk together – a reporter walking and talking and interviewing somebody is done a really slow pace because what they're doing is not actually going anywhere but it would be a bit weird for them to stand still, so what they do is they just go for a walk on the path really slowly because what they're doing is concentrating on speaking, not walking, so that is what your dog is doing when he's walking – he's concentrating on sniffing, not on walking.

Or if you picture two cops walking a beat – they walk at that really slow pace because they have nowhere to go, they're just out patrolling the environment. So we either walk at that really, really slow pace meandering along or we start striding out which is what you see in an upcoming video.

https://youtu.be/Dp6JPrZ7hIY

So back to the video of us going down the stairs. So you'll see there that I put the treat placement in front of his nose or on the step in front of him. You don't have to do all of these things but it helps you. He does a slow stop start stop start which is difficult for him. Then you'll notice at the bottom of the stairs he gave me a nice smile and a loose lead. So he's walking happily with me now and he now does this most of the time even if I don't have food, he's learned "okay this is how we navigate a set of stairs together", so it's the same as Sam the Acrobat and I, it's quite a simple thing that you're doing there in the video. Doing a nice wee trot down the stairs and he comes with me but even then he jumps at the last step because that's easier for him. You can actually see the improvement and the evolution of it as it goes. Now remember this doesn't take very long it just requires you to do it every time you're out.

One of my clients had a little dog, she walks a mile a minute – really fast, she opens the door and it was like this blast of energy hitting me, and I asked if we could slow it all down because if that's the pace she's going out walking at with the dog no wonder he's psyched up before even get out the door! So even things as simple as breathing to slow things down, slowly reach towards them, slowly take a hold of his lead or collar or harness, clip the lead on nice and relaxed and slowly move your hand forward. Move smoothly towards the door, move slowly out – the US Marines use this: "slow is smooth and smooth is fast."

So I want to slow things down till they're nice and smooth and we have got them smooth the speed will take care of itself. If we need speed which you see in the next video. So by slowing everything down and being aware of what we are doing it will centre your dog. So rather than opening that door and being in a great rush to get to the park and playing with a ball for 20 minutes and then rushing back, that half hour that it takes you to do all of that, you could instead go for a meander around the block with your dog and you're really be giving your dog more sensory century stimulation by doing that than you would by taking a ball out and chucking it. We still need to give them the physical activities as well but people get hung up on the walk being the primary source of the dog's exercise and it should actually be about the two of you going out and doing something really, really cool together.

I spend a lot of time with my dog just going out and hanging about, we just meander around the street. If I see something interesting that he might be interested in then I'll start getting him towards that so that he then notices it and then we can go together – it might be an interesting smell, whatever. So this is really about changing our perception about what a walk actually looks like. In martial arts if you can do a movement slowly then you can do it quickly, in fact it might actually be harder to do it slowly at first but it makes you better at the move. It pays to slow everything down because that gives you the skill and that gives you the control. Secondly your environment becomes our Fun Park – stairs or grass or gravel or chuckies become part of your personal assault course. Also if you and I were going out for a walk together as human beings, I wouldn't chuck your jacket at you and hassle you out the door – it wouldn't be like that, yet so many dog owners come home from work grab the dog and haul it out the door by the neck trying to get the walk over as quickly as possible so they can tick the box and say 'hand on heart that I've walked my dog so I'm guilt free' Meanwhile the dog is completely psyched.

Going back to the martial arts analogy I've talked about this before in a video blog that I've done in the past. People are looking for an outcome, the outcome of I've taken my dog for a walk, I can tick off that check box so then you wonder why the dog is dragging them around the street. But if they concentrated on each individual part of the technique of you doing a hip throw or a shoulder throw in Judo, if you're training a new guy that new guy is desperate to throw you across his shoulder and that's why he can't move you because all he's trying to do is throw you. But if you concentrate instead on the six steps that make up a good throw in order to progress he can throw you no problem. It's having the discipline to do it.

Just imagine you are walking around a market place in France and you're on holiday and you've got your friend or partner with you and you're interested in looking at something, but instead they are constantly going "Come on come on" and you're like "I just picked this wallet up, I just want to have a look at it and I maybe want to buy it" and they're constantly hurrying you away. That's what we do with our dogs. Meanwhile the dog is thinking "hang on I'm sniffing" and they're getting hauled away by the collar and the next video we'll be looking at covers this. But I often say to my clients "can you give your dog a minute out of your life to let him investigate that smell?"

In actual fact it won't take a minute - it might take 20 or 30 seconds most of the time and even if it takes a minute, even if it takes two minutes, can you give your dog two minutes of your life to investigate a really interesting smell? So going back to the market analogy you turn round to whoever you're with and you say "Can you give me a minute to actually look at this thing because it's really nice and I want to look at it." Think about going to a museum with someone who really appreciates art, in contrast to going with somebody who doesn't appreciate art. That's not a good combination. Imagine them standing there for 45 minutes to an hour appreciating a photograph or a painting and your tapping your watch saying "come on come on, Coronation Street is on" So it's all about looking at things from your dog's point of view - it's primarily their walk. Someone is taking you out of captivity for an hour out of your day to drag you round the park and then throws you back in and you're supposed to feel grateful!

Hopefully you're starting to see more and more that it's about the relationship – the revelation is the dog is probably more trainable than the human is, this is 90 percent of human training.

https://youtu.be/cSAneM8fiak

We get to meet Susie with her dog. We are striding out here as we walk along the path so the lead is relatively short and Susie is striding out. The dog it's called Charlie and she is doing what is called an A to B walk, we are simply walking from a to B and will not stop so you see in the video he moved towards another dog and Susie continues to stride forward which is basically telling the dog 'I'm not stopping and you're going to have to keep up with me.'

Now this is not in fact the most pleasant walk for your dog but there will be times when you have to walk your dog from A to B. So imagine you're out with your two-year-old and you're going to meet a friend and you say "we've got five minutes -we need to go" and you take them by the hand and you walk as quickly as you can and your two-year-old is walking with you. They don't get to stop and go into the sweet shop or the toy shop en route. You actually say to them "we can do that another time." So this is the dog walking equivalent but it's a little bit of guidance on the lead and what cues the dog that this is happening is that the lead position is short and the pace is fast and your dog absolutely needs to learn how to do that. But for every one time that you do that, for every minute that I did that, I will be providing my dog with 10 or 15 minutes of the slow stuff to balance that out. It's important to understand why are we doing that.

If you're out with your dog and you've only taught your dog to meander with you, and you've never taught your dog to walk like this, if you get a text message or a phone call when you're out and your son's been locked out of the house. I need to get back up the road quickly or there is a flood or some other emergency, you need to go back as quickly and as easily as you both can.

You have to get from wherever you are back to base as quickly as you can. You may only have five minutes to walk your dog so you decide to go to the shop and take a dog with you. "I'm going to march down there, buy a pint of milk and get back" – that's a far better experience for your dog than being left in the house, more often or not but if you've only got five minutes you can't afford to stop and sniff all the time.

If you're walking down the street and there is another dog coming towards you, that dog may be having a hard time and maybe lunging or barking whatever, you can then help out another owner by saying I'm going to walk him past – I'm going to shorten that lead and march past, and what you do with that is the pace, you change the lead position and you look where you're going, you don't look at the hazards. It's pretty single-minded from the walker's point of you – we are going this way and you're going to come with me. And you and your dog absolutely needs to learn how to do this.

In the video you'll see the dog was checking with its owner. Is this okay? Am I doing it right? And by keeping your body position the same all the time, he's only a young dog, he's only about nine months old, the whole time he checked in with Susie as if "are we still doing this? Oh yes we are still doing that." So yes you can acknowledge him but you don't stop and pet.

Now this is as harsh as I get, but you're balancing it out against other things. If he was to stop and sniff at that point because the lead is short there's only a little bit of leeway – there's only an inch or two of slack in that lead. If he moves forward towards that you're actually just continuing to walk and the movement takes that slack in gradually – there isn't that jolt on his neck from a tight lead so in the learning stages of this, you keep that little bit of slack in the lead and your movement will take up the slack if your dog veers off course. Then he'll come back and the lead slackens off again okay?

There is no doubt in my mind that dogs don't particularly like this, but you can learn that as part of a fantastic life. See if this is as bad as it gets occasionally then that's what I subscribe to – that's as harsh as it gets for the dog and in this great life yes I'm going to put my dog through that. The problem that we have is, if we start that training with the dog that is only six or eight or 18 months old   And the dog has only ever been allowed to do anything it wants that's now putting rules into a being that's never been bound by rules before and that is horrible for the dog. It's the same as with my dog Logan I don't do that type of walk with him because it will be too unpleasant for him because I didn't do that with him at the start but now I've started to do that type of work because he's had all that background.

The earlier this starts the better - with the puppies you need to be incredibly careful doing that because they don't have the physical capability to do that while they're only young weeks old so it's about being super careful. So how you would start that with the puppy is that as the puppy moves forward I would stand still and keep that dog on a short but slack lead. He moves 2 inches forward there is nowhere to go. You've started the process of saying to the dog 'you don't get to do what you want every single time that you want to do it.' We have a client just now who is a real hippy so everything in his mind is like this wonderful life for his dog and what we said to him is you're not the only person in society. One time his dog ran off and there was a man in his 60s with a big poodle and the poodle was bouncing up and down as this wee dog was running around and that's the impact that your behaviour has on somebody else because you've not enforced rules on your dog. That impacts on other people and that's not fair because we are living in a society in a shared space. Our dog's behaviour shouldn't have a negative impact on somebody else and their dog

https://youtu.be/be5Z-mugUDU

Next video in this chapter you see some movement drills – just a little bit of fun stuff and again that a number of things: we have the bollards there that we can weave in and out of and I'm walking up and down over them and all I'm doing is just another exercise to teach him how to move with me. So we go up and over all of the benches and then you get a treat at the end for staying with me. But when we first started doing this as you saw in the earlier videos I was having to do a lot more reinforcement, whereas he is now thinking that it's cool and because he is quite a physical dog this can be reinforcement in itself. He is built to move. The bollards that you can see in the video, we could be moving in and out of them in a bigger way, getting him to move backwards and forwards – it's just a little bit of fun.

This approach to dog training I believe benefits everybody - it's a win/win. Remember that the dog is an equal, it's not a trophy, it's not a pet, and it's not an inconvenience that you grudgingly have to spend time with. If that's your attitude then sorry but maybe you shouldn't have one. They are a member of your family and they are a living, sentient being who has needs and we need to take care of those needs.

If you were to implement just some of the stuff your dog would have a better quality of life and be happy so if you do more with your dog, your dog will want to do more with you. It's the same as in any relationship just as I said before - the more stuff that you do with the other being/person/dog in that relationship that the dog likes, the more he or she will want to spend time with you and that's what you're looking for ultimately.

CHAPTER THREE– AGGRESSIVE BEHAVIOUR

In this chapter we're going to talk about how dog owners who maybe have dogs that are pulling on the lead, or being aggressive, or jumping up on people can be transformed into beloved, happy little furry friends in about 15 minute of a day.

We're gonna talk about dog-to-dog aggression, which is very common behaviour problem that I deal with, and it probably is about ... conservatively, this or some aspect of this accounts for at least 40% of the work that I do. So dogs having a go at other dogs.

Now you might be wondering do customers and things come to me saying, "I've got an aggressive dog," or is it something I tend to notice once I start working with people?

Very often what we'll do is if they email me and are looking for some help, they'll have already have identified that the dog has shown aggressive, or it's now described as reactive, behaviours, towards other dogs. Probably about 10 years ago, we started to describe it as reactivity, but basically it's an aggressive display, so it's usually lunging and barking at other dogs and lunging and barking uncontrollably at other dogs, so it's not just very often that they'll lunge and bark, it's that they'll lunge and bark and not stop.

It can be an extremely stressful behavior to live with if your dog is showing that because it takes away a lot of the joy of what most people have of their daily lives with their dogs, and taking it to the nth degree, it can be that people can't take their dog out the garden, so the dog spends most of the time in the garden or they'll walk their dog at half past five, six o'clock in the morning or at midnight in order to avoid everybody else, so that there's no chance that we're gonna run into other dogs. It can have a ... Not can. It does have a significant impact on the people who are living with this problem.

So is it something that can be changed easily or is this more of a long-term thing?

It can be changed fairly readily in most cases. With most cases, you will see a difference in working with that dog within the first hour, just by explaining to the person what their dog is trying to achieve and then how to try and meet those needs. The first hour just very often we have a wee bit of a light bulb moment with the clients when they understand that the behavior is not in the dog, the behavior is in the environment the dog is in, which we've spoken about before, and once they understand that there's lots that they can do to change that environment, which we'll talk about over the course of this chapter, and putting that into play fairly readily, and we also have to look at the owner's history of being reinforced.

The reason why they behave in a certain way is because they're anxious, scared, terrified, apprehensive, or anything along those spectrum of emotions of the dog getting into a fight with another dog, of the embarrassment of it, the dog may be biting somebody or another dog. They've got all that to live with, and very often the handling that they do gets in the way of the dog making progress, and it's generally tight-lead handling, stiff bodies and holding their breath, and all those things now become just a whole series of cues to the dog that this is not a cool situation. The first hour, very often, we'll spend some time just trying to take pressure off both the dog and the owner so that everybody can relax, and then when we're relaxed, we can learn.

Is there any such thing, then, as an aggressive dog, or is there more to it?

Well, again, it depends. Would you say that there's an aggressive person? Some people are more prone to be aggressive, but if you don't put them in a situation where they're likely to be aggressive then they're not gonna be aggressive. Aggression is not a bad thing; it's just a bad thing if that's what you do all the time.

Very often it's an extremely useful set of behaviours to have because it keeps us safe, that's the purpose of it. Aggressive displays are there to make sure you don't get into a fight, and then if you do get into a fight, the more aggressive you are, the more likely you are to survive, so from an evolutionary point of view, it has served most species. What we're really talking about is inappropriate aggression, and without getting too philosophical within ... I mean, we could have a big discussion on what's appropriate and what's not, but that's for another time. What we're really talking about is your dog displaying aggressive behaviours in situations where the bulk of the dog population wouldn't express the same behaviours or exhibit those same behaviours.

So this can range from violent barking, excited vocalization, pulling on a lead, bouncing up and down, lunging backwards and forwards, lunging forwards, to biting, and really that's what we're talking about. We'd have to identify or describe the behaviours that we're talking about, but we're really talking about that set of behaviours. Growling, lunging, barking, snapping and biting towards other dogs and people. People are slightly different from this because there's different things that we need to do, but it's very, very, very similar when you're treating both sets of behaviours.

The worst I have ever seen with this was a big bull lurcher, so bull lurchers are greyhound crossed with some sort of bull breed, so they're generally like a greyhound but big head, more muscular. Extremely powerful, and this dog could not see another dog at a hundred yards without going doolally.

I mean, really lunging and barking and baying at the end of the lead, not able to relax, and the closer the dog got, the worse the behavior got, so there's a pretty unmanageable dog, and lots and lots and lots of management and that, and what we also have to look at as well is ... you then start having to look at the ethics of putting a dog who is that aggressive through a stressful training program. Regardless of how kind the methods I'm using, where you could, with lots of stuff, fairly easily manage that dog's environment to make sure the dog isn't running into other dogs, and that would be in extreme cases like that. It may be necessary to walk the dog at six o'clock in the morning or at midnight, putting them in the car and taking them away to someone, a secure dog run and exercise the dog there, but out of the 4,000-odd hours of client-facing time I've had, that's one dog. They're so rare that actually we should really only be talking about them amongst professionals, really.

What I'm gonna do first is I'm gonna go through... I made some notes here, so we're really just dipping our toe into this, so I've got a six-week course on issues like this for owners, and we do four classroom inputs and then two practical inputs, and the reason why, when you go through the stuff that you actually have to learn when you're dealing with dogs like this, it's pretty mammoth. It's one of the reasons why actually we're only just skimming the surface of this, because dealing with aggression should be done by people who are skilled and experienced with dealing with these issues.

I was "fortunate", and I'll put that word in quotes, that when I started this, we were using old-school training methods, using choke chains, and metal collars and stuff like that. My two mastiffs, who were my first dogs back in 2000, 2003 when I first got them. They were big dogs that became aggressive towards other dogs, so that was before I started into dog training professionally. That's the reason, fundamentally, why I am here. If it hadn't been for those dogs, we might not be having this conversation. I'd be away doing something else, probably. I already had some skills, living with these dogs on a day-to-day basis, and then my previous job was in the police before, and I didn't realize how many transferable skills that I had from being in the police to dealing with aggressive dogs.

You're just dealing with an aggressive being, a member of another species, and so when I designed this six-week course, when I sat down and broke down all the skills that you have, it's pretty mammoth, actually, and the six-week course that we do, we do four two-hour classroom inputs, and then we do some practical work at the end, and that's so that the owners will get some sort of knowledge as to what they're doing before they then start working in an environment where their dog is gonna display aggressive behaviours because it's such a ... the potential for it to go wrong. Sorry, what can potentially happen when it goes wrong is serious, whereas if you're training a friendly dog, and if you call and a dog doesn't come back to you, and you're in a public park or something like that, there's not an awful lot that can go wrong.

I'll go through a few things. There's a six-point training plan, and that's credited to Eva Bertilsson and Emelie Johnson Vegh who are two trainers from Sweden. They have a six-point training plan, so what they'll say is what are the goals for my dog's behavior? What's the plan to get there? What's the goal for our own behavior, so what do we need to do? What's the plan for us to learn those skills and those behaviours? We then need to train ourselves to do those skills, and then we need to train the dog. That's a lot.

That's what we actually should be doing before we even put our hands on a dog, but people are living with these problems on a day-to-day basis, so we need to try and give them something that they can do within the space of an hour, which you'll see in the videos that we're gonna show.

Rules for aggression reduction. You need to understand the scenarios under which your dog will display aggressive behaviours, and always be ready for that scenario to take place and for the aggression to take place if those factors are in play. Recognize the precursors, so that's things like growling, the dog lifting his lips and baring his teeth. You can quite often get the dog showing his teeth without growling, so he'll just start doing this. Very often what has happened is by the time the dog comes to us, the person has started punishing those behaviours, so what happens is the dog shows those behaviours, and we now chastise them and tell them "no". Those are the warning behaviours that we really want to be looking out for. There's a bunch of warning behaviours that happen even before then, so the dog will generally try and disengage, generally will try and walk away. If the dog approaches them or the person approaches them they will generally try to leave, but because they're on a lead and we don't recognize what's going on, we don't allow them that space to leave.

What happens is that those precursors are the warnings signs that the dog is not happy have been suppressed through telling a dog "no", correcting the dog, or whatever. What you're now doing is you've not removed the dog's needs for the space from the scary dog or person, but what you've done is you've removed the ability for the dog to tell you that they're not happy. That is a big one. We then need to use redirection or apply an appropriate training strategy, so redirect a dog onto doing something else or put in play a training strategy that we've got when you recognize those precursors.

Wee bit of slamming the stable door here, but stop or avoid the situation before it starts, and that means from the early stages, so while you've got your young dog, or your puppy, or your adolescent dog, is to recognize all those precursors and then do something about it at that stage, but that is a wee bit too late for what we're talking about here, and then try and keeping records of what we're doing so that you know what progression we're making.

There's two ways that we can ... Once a being on this planet has learned a behavior, we can't unlearn it, so you can get less practiced at. If I was to ask you how long you've been driving a car for for, how long have you been driving? Let's say at least 30 years. Okay. You will never unlearn that, unless, God forbid, you got dementia, but we're not talking about that. I'm not being disrespectful there. Unless there's some sort of physical degradation in your brain, you're never gonna unlearn that, because you've been driving for 30 years, but if you haven't driven for a year, your driving skills will be rustier than they are tomorrow. We wanna try and put roadblocks.

There's two strategies. Once a dog has learned that an aggressive response gets the outcome that they want, and we've talked about that previously. Generally aggression is to tell the thing that the dog is being aggressive to go away. That's a broad generalization, but it happens in most cases. You get some dogs that actually like a bit of a fight, and they just get a buzz from it, and then you've also got predatory behavior, so the dog is ... they're actually not being aggressive, they're hunting at that point, and that's slightly different. It's a different mind-set.

We're talking in the main about dogs that are using an aggressive display to try and repel the oncoming dog or person. Okay?

Once the dog has learnt that that's a strategy that works, they can't unlearn it. It's always gonna be in their behavioural repertoire. There's two ways that we can do it. There's two ways that we can change their behavior. We can either constantly suppress that response through punishment, so that would be always correcting the dog, always being on top of the dog, using leash corrections, metal collars, electric collar, rattle cans and all that stuff, which we don't use. That's one way that you can do it. But what the fallout with that is when you stop doing that, the aggression will now start coming back up because you've not trained a replacement behavior to achieve the same result. All that you've done is just keep smashing that behavior down, and when you stop it, it'll start popping back up again. That's the first way, which we don't do.

The other way is that you start teaching the dog different behaviours in order to achieve the same result, and you build skills and confidence in the dog that that result isn't necessary in the first place. I'm not lunging and barking because I'm frightened. I'm lunging and barking, and I'm frightened because the dog is too close to me. If the person is not too close to me or the dog is not too close to me, I won't lunge and bark. If I'm not frightened by their presence, I won't lunge and bark. Those are the two elements that we can use in order to change the dog's behavior. That's really what we're looking at, and that's what we spend quite a lot of our time explaining to people. If you just give yourself distance from the scary dog or scary person and let the dog watch, the dog will now offer behaviours which are reinforceable, so the absence of an unwanted behavior for the purposes of what we are doing has to be a wanted behavior.

If you hold a dog back, which you'll see in some of the videos, and give the dog other things to do, they now start going, "Oh, I can see that dog and not go nuts." That now gives us an opportunity to reinforce those behaviours because we can't do nothing, so just now ... Logan, my dog, is who you'll see in some of the videos. He is lying sleeping on the couch. That's what he's doing just now. He's not doing nothing. He can't do nothing. He's alive.

Even if he gets up and stands in front of me, he's not doing nothing. He's standing in front of me looking at something.

Okay? And those are now behaviours that I can reinforce if I so desire. That's the first part. We'll go onto some of the video in a second, okay, because there's a few other notes. The skills that the handler needs to learn or be aware of: observing the environment, observing the dog's body language and understanding what that means, anticipating what is about to change in the environment based on what is happening, be aware of our movement and know how to move, know how to handle the lead sympathetically to the dog, identifying what reinforcement we're gonna use. Well, that's food, toys or space from that other dog. Blocking our dog from following through on a potentially unwanted behavior, and that would be done with a lead, so the dog would move forward and you need to learn how to block them safely on the lead. Being able to make a dynamic risk assessment about what's going on, and being able to do all that in a dynamically changing environment. This is a massive skillset for people to learn, so it's ... When I actually sat and broke that down like that, this is a lot, which is why it's only experienced, skilled people who should be doing it and offer advice on it.

But we want to offer some advice so that somebody can go away today and go, "I can try that and I can try that safely." The skills that your dog needs to learn is they need to be able to accept blocking, so if they move towards the end of the lead, they need to be able to accept that when that lead becomes tight, or their harness, that's as far as they can move, and understand that that's as far as they can move. They need to be able to move within the range of the lead and move with the handler as the handler's moving, and we'll hopefully see that in ... We'll see some good examples and some not so good examples in the video.

Switch from one activity to another, and that's about engaging different parts of the brain. If your dog is eyeballing another dog, that's not compatible with sniffing and searching the ground. Sniffing and searching the ground is a seeking behavior and the emotion there is curiosity, whereas eyeballing another dog is not a seeking and searching behavior, that's a safety behavior, if you like. The emotion that goes with that is wariness, anxiety, whatever we want to talk about and whatever would we label that.

Switching from one activity to the next, and the more you can build that up in your dog, the easier they're able to get to do these skills, and to be able to discriminate what's important in an environment and what's not, so you can do lots of things with even just clicker training your dog in your living room to do a whole bunch of ... If you trained five behaviours and a dog is able to bang them out first time, so if you ask a dog to sit, stand, lie down, roll over one way and roll over the other on five verbal cues, the dog has now started picking up the skill of being able to discriminate. That's important and that's not ... Again, listen for the words. These are things that you can do. A dog who has got more skills is generally easier to work with than dog that doesn't.

Now that you're blown away by everything that you're gonna have to do if you're living with a dog who is showing reactive behaviours, we can start looking at some of the videos, and it's just so that you understand what's actually going on there. We'll watch the first video.

https://www.youtube.com/watch?v=j6ch7h1MOds

We'll just watch it first, and then I'll talk through it.

Ally is the dog and I can't remember what the client's name is. I apologize. But Ally's a dog, and she's recently been adopted, so she came in from Europe, which is why she's got no tail and those cocked ears, and she's just young. She's only about 10 months old, and she shows these behaviours that we talk about, so she pulls forward on the end of the lead when she sees another dog, bounces backwards and forwards and lunges and barks.

What we've done at first is we've provided them with the safety that she needs through using an appropriate distance, so you can see John and Millie in the background. John, and Millie is a Labrador, so we're using those. Now, because I know John and he goes to the park every morning, I know that Millie's gonna stay around John and not come in towards us. We're holding at that distance, and now when she looks, we're allowing her to look at Millie because she needs to know where she is in order to make assessments of whether she's safe or not. This is not a, "Look at me, look at me, look at me." This is allowing your dog to look, if she wants to.

If you are terrified of snakes and you're sitting here just now and I'm watching you, and I see a big snake slithering down your bookcase, and I'm going, "No, look at me, look at me," and you can see it in the camera, you want to turn around and look at that so that you can move away, or if it starts sliding out the door, to go further back into the room. What I tend to do is allow the dog to look at the scary thing, person or dog, at a distance that they feel safe, or at least show non-aggressive behaviors. Now we're reinforcing that with food. Food's a good choice here because she likes it and she'll take it, but what we might do with other dogs is when she looks at the dog and looks back at us, we might walk away and give her more safety, more quiet behavior.

Now, the other thing in this is what happens here is ... you see there Millie runs and Ally picks up. She goes from sitting to standing and she looks at the dog. She then turns around and starts jumping. She's jumping because she doesn't know what else to do, and jumping has had a high history of previous reinforcement, so if Ally doesn't know what to do, she'll jump on a person because historically that has given her access to some reinforcement, whether it's petting, being told to get down, getting pushed, to be pushed away or whatever. So it's called resurgence, and that is very often what we see. That's just information for us that Ally doesn't have enough reinforcement history doing other behaviours in those circumstances, and it means that we don't need to get annoyed with the dog that the dog's jumping on us.

Okay. What we've said to her is, "You've had your look, and we're gonna go." Because we're moving away from the other dogs, we're actually giving her more of what she wants. That was a really nice example of when lots of things go right.

The lead was slacking as well. Let's see an example of this. Okay. To make a cup of tea, making a cup of tea is the behavior. The factors that need to be in play are access to kettle, access to tea, access to milk and sugar if you like it, access to electricity, and a cup. Those five things have to take place for the behavior of making tea to be able to occur. If the electricity is off, there's no tea being made, but as soon as you put all those factors together, you'll get tea-making, if you want a cup of tea.

Very often what we get is it's not just the distance from the other dog, it is distance from other dog, tension in the lead, owner holding their breath, other dog moving, other dog moving towards us. You could actually sit there and look at ... there might be six factors in play, and by changing a few of those factors, we now change the behavior because we're not allowing the circumstances to happen which the dog has previously learnt have to take place before tea-making can occur.

Very often what happens is the dog is doing fine, and the handler will pick up the lead and start putting tension, and that alone will now cause the dog to kick off. What I do there is if I'm putting tension in the lead, and you see that there. There's just a little bit. The lead lifts up and she feels a tiny bit of pressure. If that happens, any time that happens, what we are always doing is walking away from another dog. What we're doing is although we're putting tension in the lead, we're increasing the distance rather than putting tension in the lead and either holding or reducing the distance. Again, we're still changing factors which allow more wanted behavior to occur.

Right, so that's the first one. This is me. The next video is me walking the boy, so problem child. What I'm doing here is I know there's gonna be dogs here, and what I'm doing is I'm building up a history with Logan in this environment of doing a different behavior. The behavior here is searching for the food, so he is now starting to practice another behavior in that environment, because I know a dog's gonna appear, because it's Sunday afternoon, and it's a nice day, and people are out with their dogs. Wee bit of ham-fisted lead handling from me there. What I'm doing there is I'm just putting some treats on the ground and giving him something else to do. Okay. Here he starts going, "Oh, this is a cool thing. I can do something else."

This dog, when I first got him, one, he wouldn't sniff outside at all, and two, wouldn't take food outside because he was that switched on all the time, and he still has his moment, but we're making progress with him. Nice relaxed body language from me, nice relaxed lead-handling, and then moving with him. All right?

Again, it's about you being aware, again, the owner, client, being aware of the environment, aware of the possible risk factors, and aware of the dog. You're engaged.

We're in the moment.

A client yesterday, we were working with him, and the dog did something which he typically does around dogs, and he then starts telling me that the dog typically does that. Now, I fully understand why he needs to tell me that, but what he's now doing is he's referring to a moment in the past, and he's not present, and I said to him, "We'll hear about it in two seconds. We'll concentrate on this just now. We'll get this, because we need to be here. Now we can go away, give the dog a break, and you can tell me what you needed to tell me," because he clearly needs to tell me or he wouldn't be talking, but there's a time and a place for that, so that's why we absolutely need to be present, but in all dog training, we need to be present. We need to be here. Here and now with our dog.

Then the second one here. The dog starts moving in. Dog's gonna come from the left-hand side of the screen.

https://www.youtube.com/watch?v=YSKEK20SjfE&feature=youtu.be

Yeah, so you see him there? Now, although he can't see him directly, there's holes in the bushes and he can see the person. Again, I put some more food on the ground to see if he can take it. I'm not distracting him here. I'm allowing him to look like that. You see the wee dog there, on the path? We're starting to get too close here, which is why I start backing off, and now I move him. I give him a second because he's gonna be okay, and then I go, "That's good, and I'm just gonna move you out of there."

Now, this is a nice bit from him here. Although he's switched on, he now starts checking in with me, and then I'm able to reinforce it again. Allow him to look. That's what he used to do before. We are too close here, but he's then able to go back to sniffing the ground. I'm saying to him, "Can you do this?" And he says, "Yeah, I can." Some things he can and some things he can't. I was over the moon with him at the weekend when I shot this. It was really, really ... Then he looks again, and then he goes back to doing what he was doing. He's starting to build up patterns of behavior, or experience, rather, that he can do other things in the presence of dogs. He doesn't need to eyeball them, and lunge and bark, and act like a lunatic.

Has another look around, and then goes back to sniffing. That's massive progress for him. I put that video up on my Facebook page, and another trainer had commented on saying that the reason he's not engaging with me is because I'm not active enough, so what we're wanting to do when we're ... You see in the first video with the Doberman, there's lots of interaction backwards and forwards between us, between the handler or the person and the dog, so there's lots of involvement from the person. What we're doing there is we're basically giving the dog lots of instruction about how they need to behave.

What I'm trying to do here with Logan, and we need to do both of these because your dog needs to be able to do both of them. There I'm trying to let him set up the environment that he can do lots of it on his own, so I am absolutely looking for him to go, "There's a dog. Who cares? I can do this. Back to sniffing." It's then he's becoming more empowered, because he can go, "I can control my own space here. If I want to, I can just turn and walk away and Dad will come with me."

We need to do both approaches, and the reason why we need to do both approaches is because the second video with Logan there teaches him how to get better. The first video shows really how now to make him any worse, or Ally worse, so if it is getting hairy, so say in the first video with the Doberman, one of those dogs had broken away from the group they were in and started coming towards us, Ally needs to have the skills of working with a person so that the person can then say, "Come on, let's go," and understand what that means, understand how to move, et cetera, et cetera, which is all the skills that we talked about in the first instance.

https://www.youtube.com/watch?v=Fh7rCK7oQUA&feature=youtu.be

Every time he disengages or looks away from these dogs, we're gonna acknowledge or hold him here. Lovely, and just balancing himself there. That's nice. Gentle, without putting any pressure on that lead, walk towards me, and he should come with you here. Lovely, and then walk back towards me. There we go. Nice. Just slow down and give him a second. Just more information about the family there.

Similar to what we were doing with Logan there. Hudson's a boxer, and him and Malcolm have got a really lovely relationship. They work really well together, but what has happened is up until we started working together was Malcolm was doing lots of physical prevention and he's doing lots of the work, and what we want to do is Hudson to be going, "Yeah, it's just dogs." The dog walkers who are in front of us who walked past with their Labradors and their retrievers, we allow Hudson to walk, and then we say to him, "Are we ready to go?" Initially he said yes, and then he comes back round and says, "I'm not finished yet," and it was because another family started walking down from the left-hand side of the screen at the back of the skateboard park, and I think that he wants to look at them to satisfy himself that there's not another dog before he turns his back on them.

If we needed to there, we would have shortened that lead up and quickly and smoothly moved off to say to him, "Cool, I'm gonna take the decision-making out of your hands now. I will decide because I have read lots of different stuff. You might be getting too stressed." Whatever. And we move him away, but it was safe for us to do there, and if you just play it again, it was safe for us to just let Hudson come in and have another look.

https://www.youtube.com/watch?v=Jq7EKBwsPbk&feature=youtu.be

The reason why we started walking away with him is because his body language started getting higher, if you like. Basically, and this is not particularly technical, more. His body language got more, so it got more stiff, more intense, more upright, more ears forwards, and he started more movement towards the dogs. Now, when all those things are in play from your dog's body language. I'm saying to him, "We're not doing that now. If you're gonna approach a dog, you're gonna approach that dog with loose, relaxed behavior, because that's how you should be approaching a dog."

We're giving him plenty of opportunity there to make decisions. If he made the wrong decision, we then said, "We're not doing that. We're gonna move six feet, eight feet away, and we're gonna see if you can do it there." Now, when you watch ... You can see before and after videos on a television, or if you were to search on YouTube for them. This is not sexy training, so it's not seeing a dog kicking off and miraculously doing something about it. What we actually should be doing here is ... I say to the clients I work with. The magic happens when the dog is not showing aggressive behaviours, because those are the behaviours that we want.

With Hudson there, we're not ready to go there until he shows more relaxed behaviours, and we get more relaxed behaviours by doing more practice of this. Now, with Ally, the Doberman, she showed fairly, and again, it's on a sliding scale, fairly relaxed behavior, and able to focus on her person at that distance from Millie. If she's able to do it at 25 yards, with practice she's able to do it at 24, 22, 21, 19, okay, but you don't keep chipping away. You don't make it more and more and more difficult each time.

What time is you make it a little bit more challenging and then you back off and start again, and then a little bit more challenging, then back off and start again, and you're basically, over time, you're chipping away at that distance. When you learn how to drive a car, first lesson you'll rarely get out of second gear, but if you can put your car in gear and make it go forward, you can drive your car at 100 miles an hour. You just need to learn all the steps in between. We don't start then. There's more a skillset for it.

First lesson, nothing sexy.

When we're dealing with aggressive dogs, a successful training session is when everything goes smoothly. It's just the dog is nice and relaxed, and pottering about, and seeing the dog and then either moving towards or moving away in a relaxed fashion. The other thing I just wanted to briefly talk about is called trigger stacking. We might have talked about it with the barking chapter.

Trigger stacking is where a series of stressors, which on their own wouldn't cause the dog to react aggressively, happen either all together or in such quick succession that the dog doesn't have time to cool off. The example I use is it's the end of May. in Scotland, actually, when we get that two weeks of summer, so it was like 75 or 80 degrees, and it's Saturday morning. We've got a nice, relaxed weekend ahead of us, and you're in your shorts and your sandals, and you're driving to the supermarket to go and buy your barbecue, and as you drive in, somebody steals your parking space, and you go, "Okay," and you just drive around, or you drive further along, and you park somewhere else.

That's in a really low stress environment. Everything is going well. Money in the bank, you're speaking to your missus, your kids are well behaved. Everything is going well in your life, and you go, "Yeah, who cares?" Now what it is, its two days before Christmas. You've just had to get two new tyres for your car, so that's £400-odd, whatever it is. Three, £400 that you didn't think that you were gonna have to spend two days before Christmas. You're loaded with a cold. Your boss is shouting at you because there's a deadline which you'd not met yet. You'd not got the turkey. You've not slept the night before because you don't feel well, and the sleet is hitting your windscreen horizontally, and you're driving to Tesco car park, and somebody steals your parking space, and all of a sudden you just explode.

That's trigger stacking to the nth degree. What we get is a good training session, and this is why even if when you did that intro with the 15 minutes, we can work on your dog's aggressive behavior in 15 minute chunks. What you would really want to do is do a little bit, and then back off, and give your dog something cool to do, and then come back and do a little bit more, and then back off again, and what you're trying to do is keep that temperature down. The other analogy that I give is say if your dog hits 100 degrees, that's when he'll show this big aggressive response. Most social dogs, okay, same as with most social people, they probably meander through life most of the time sitting at about 40 degrees, so even if their temperature doubles, they're only going up to 80. That's hot for them, but it's well below boiling point. You hit 80 degrees and then you cool off again, and you've got the ability to cool off because you've got so much other good stuff going on in your life.

What happens when we work with dogs like these is you bring them to the park and the dog's already at 60 degrees or 70 degrees before you even get in there, because the dog's anticipating, "I'm gonna meet dogs in this environment because I've always met dogs in this environment before." You see your first dog, and the dog goes up to 75 degrees, and you do really well. The dog goes up to 75, you do everything cool. Reinforce all those behaviours, and you either keep him at 75 or you bring him back down to 72. You're now two degrees heavier than the baseline was, but in the park. You now see another dog and you go up to 77, and then you come back down to 75, and then you go up to 80, back down to 77, up to 82, 83, back down to 80. You see how over the course of an hour, if you're not giving your dog enough opportunity to cool off, it just builds a little bit more, a little bit more, a little bit more, a little bit more, and then after 40 minutes, the dog's just like, "Ah, I've had enough. Get me out of here."

Now, when one is learning how to do this, the tendency for us, it becomes so reinforcing for us that your dog is now showing relaxed behaviours in the environment where it would ordinarily show aggressive behaviors, so that's massively reinforcing for us, which means we're gonna do more of it. What happens is you're like that. "One more round, I'm just gonna get another round in," and what you should be doing is doing a few less rounds. If you're at the stage when you're working a with dog like this that you think the dog's had enough, make a note of the time that you've been out and the number of exposures you've had, and see the next time you come out, stop 10 minutes before that, because we don't want a dog just to be on the cusp all the time.

We want a dog to leave with all those good experiences, so with the video with me with Logan, with me putting the food down into the grass, I go at quiet times and I build lots of experience in those environments doing cool things so that he's now not expecting ... He looks around, there's no dogs. Cool. Okay. We'll spend 20 minutes, half an hour just bumbling around, searching for food, I clap him and then I take him home, and he goes like that, "That was really nice," and I go, "I know. It was, wasn't it?" Right, so the next time we come back there, he's got some reference to being outside in a public space where he can smell dogs and go, "That was tight. Cool. Yeah, that was cool."

Again, it's just a brief introduction to give people an idea of what kind of things are involved in working with a dog who's showing aggressive behaviours, and the one thing that I would say, the single biggest factor in this that I have found is distance from the stressor, so distance from a dog or the person, and if you can create that distance that the dog needs and he's then showing non-aggressive behaviours, you have now got behaviours that you reinforce, and over time if you can just start chipping away at that, and that's something that somebody who is relatively unskilled can do relatively easily and relatively often.

If you're going to the gym because you wanna lose fat or build some muscle, you're gonna record how many reps you did, and what kind of weight you did and what machine you did. You're there to train. You're not there to whine and bitch and socialize. And you keep records. People keep records, they break records. If you care about your dog and you want your relationship to be great, and you wanna have fun with that animal for as long as you possibly can, you've dragged this animal on that chain. It's like dragging a phobic person on a chain into a room full of snakes, and then when you try and get away, you yank the chain and go, "No, you're not doing that." What do you think's gonna happen?

It's very interesting. Again, the same theme of ... and it's a synergistic relationship.

And just the other thing as well is about your record-keeping, and this is where people start ... We've talked about this before as well. I'm pretty sure we did the last time. We've got a scenario A, and scenario A has seven factors which then cause the dog to show aggressive behaviours. Under scenario A, with those seven factors, your dog will show aggression 100% of the time, for this example. We now have scenario A minus one, so minus one of those factors, and your dog is now not showing aggressive behaviours or only showing aggressive behaviours 90% of the time. That's a 10% improvement with one change.

Now, if you change a number of those factors, you now get a bigger chunk of improvement. Say for talking's sake, scenario A, prior to training, 100% of the time the dog will show aggressive behaviours. With time it now goes to 90, 80, 70, 60, and so on. Now if I made those gains, if I made a 10% improvement or 20% or 30% improvement at the gym this week, I'd be delighted, but firstly it doesn't happen like that.

Now, what happens is when it gets into the small numbers, so if we think about it, 100% of the time is seeing 100 dogs and your dog will kick off. 90% of the time now means seeing 90 out of 100 and the dog will kick off. 80%, and so on. Now what happens is that you may go ... When you get into 1%, that means for every hundred dogs you see, your dog only reacts aggressively to one of them, and now you've got that, "What the hell happened there? He was doing so well." He's still doing well, because he's only reacting aggressively one in a hundred, whereas before it was 100 out of 100. Then it goes to one in 150, one in 200, one in 250. You see how the behavior is diminishing, but not entirely going away. It's just getting less and less and less, and we're getting longer and longer and longer between reactive episodes or aggressive episodes, and those are the ones that our eye is drawn towards, and you now start going back to your previous patterns of behavior, which then opens the door, the roadblock which you have previously set up, and your dog just belts down that motorway of the aggressive behaviours, and now you get to your four or five incidents in a row.

All that you've done now, and I say that to the client. "Look at the numbers." They'll come back to me after a couple of months and say, "He's reacted six times in the last week," and I say, "Cool. In the last two months, how many times has your dog reacted aggressively?" And they'll say, "10," and I say, "And six of those have been in the last week?" "Yep." The first thing we'll do is has there been change to your routine, has there been change to the amount of exercise he's getting, to what they've been feeding him, to where he's been sleeping, or whatever. That's the first thing we would rule out, and then what I say to them, "Although it's been six in the last week, it's been 10 in the last two months, whereas before in the last two months prior to you working with me it would have been in the hundreds and hundreds and it's now been 10. Cool. That's fine. Let's just get back on the wagon and keep doing what we were doing, and those numbers will start tailing off again."

Then the big improvements are then when your dog will react aggressively one in 500 times or one in 1000 times, and see when we get into those numbers, that's now within the normal parameters of what would you have expected it to be an aggressive response for most members of a species living in a society with those species, and I say this to clients as well. "In the drive here today, how many times did you shout at another driver?" Some of them will say none, and I say, "Cool. I've shouted at three people for undue hesitancy at a junction."

That's an aggressive display, but if I was reacting like that every single interaction I would be having, that's not cool. But you might just think he's a wee bit of a hot head and he shouts occasionally when he's driving. Most people do that, and it's okay. Obviously we would want to do less of that, but it's still within a normal expression of human behavior.

Aggression in dogs towards other dogs or any other living animal is ... I suppose you could call it an extreme behavior. It's a nightmare scenario, and it makes sense that it's gonna take a bit of work to get it done, but, as ever, I think watching the way I work and watching the ... it's a two-way relationship. For the living in the now, and you being aware of the environment and being aware of the triggers. You have to go out on a limb because that's where the fruit is, you know?

If you want the big reward, you want the big gain, you need to do the work. But it's a fantastic relationship. Fantastic relationship-building exercise, and at the end of the day, isn't that the reason why you've got the animal in the first place?

You're providing your dog with what they need, and if you're providing them with the food that they need, the shelter they need, the medical care that they need, why wouldn't you provide them with their emotional needs as well, which might be, "Please don't put me in towards that dog. I don't like them." You wouldn't do that with your partner or your child. "I don't wanna go to that party. It's full of people that I don't like." Cool. We don't need to go. Okay?

Notice in the video the owner is always moving towards the animal, which is just slacking the lead. Moving in to take that pressure off the lead, yeah, so that we're not walking the dog back, and the dog got to that space. We let them get there, so I think it's fair we take two steps or a half-step towards them to do that, rather than pulling a dog back in and leaving the pressure off, okay?

We let the dog get there, so we really need to do the work, because if you're shorting the lead up and holding there, while you've still got slack, you wouldn't need to move your feet. You think, if you're not slack, because you're standing right next to them and you've got a couple of feet of slack left.

Again if you're reading this and you're motivated, you're inspired, you're liking what you hear, but you want some expert guidance on it, remember that you can email me through my website, which is glasgowdogtrainer.co.uk, or direct email is info@glasgowdogtrainer.co.uk. I'm on Facebook as Glasgow Dog Trainer and Behavior Consultant. You can contact me through there. Most of my videos are on YouTube as well as Facebook, and that's Glasgow Dog Trainer on YouTube, and the course on aggression that we've basically just done a tiny introduction to in this chapter, next year I'll be getting that online so that people can come on and look at the eight, 10 hours of learning on that as well, and that's basically just going into what we've done here but in more depth, and a lot more than that as well.

I hope this has been useful to you. Get in touch. Share this stuff. I'm easy to find on the web, and benefit from it. You and your animal will be grateful for it at the end of the day.

CHAPTER FOUR – NUISANCE BARKING

Welcome to chapter four, where we are going to be talking about the subject of nuisance barking.

Doggy barking at all the wrong times, at all the wrong things.

And it's only nuisance barking for the owner, it's not nuisance barking for the dog.

Oh, that is a critical distinction right there. Yeah, nuisance according to who? Okay, so you want an obedient and reliable, trustworthy pet, but as we have established, over the time that we have spent together in this book, is very much a symbiotic relationship. Sometimes, it is just about as much training the human as it is training the animal.

So why does this come up? How often does this come up, and why is it such a big deal?

It comes up fairly often, and when we did our survey asking our clients and fans what the top five or six problems that bothered them were, nuisance barking was within those top five. I would generally, describe it from what my clients are telling me, as bark-just as you said there, barking at inappropriate moments or times, and they continue to bark at that amount of time for-continuing to bark. Rather than, just barking, and then stopping.

In maybe... three or four appointments a fortnight, but it also comes up as a symptom of other stuff. The aggression work, or aggression reactivity that we are going to talk about next time, and nuisance barking very often becomes as an element of that. What we are going to talk about this chapter, is just barking that annoys us, or barking at the window, barking at television, barking at other dogs, barking to get attention, barking at the door and not stopping. Those types of things.

I remember, being at a friend's house - this was when I was a teenager, and they had a Staffordshire Bull Terrier. Whose name escapes me, but this guy was a big dude. All muscle and teeth, you know? He was routinely chained to the wall in the living room, and you had to kind of creep on around the edge of the living room just to get to the kitchen because, as I said, this thing was huge. I remember, watching the reason why he was chained to the wall was because, when another dog went past the window, he went absolutely berserk. He was still shouting about an hour later. Even though the dog was long gone. It was just unbelievable.

I think, at one point, he actually, did go through the double glazed window trying to get to the animal, but the neighbours had dogs. There was a dog down the road. There was somebody upstairs in the flat. Or, your own dogs just pissing everybody off. It comes up quite a lot.

Very often, it will just be that the dog will bark-just as I said, at these times, and the owner doesn't think that they can do anything about it. What they are doing is not working. Very often, what they will be trying to do is shouting at the dog, telling the dog to shut up, and as far as the dog is now concerned is,

"Everybody's barking now." Okay. So, I am barking. You are barking. I am barking at something outside. You are now barking at me. I will bark back at you. Everybody now, just joins in, and annoys.

The common ones, are-we will cover a couple of fairly common scenarios, that the dog barks at. The first one will be, whereas you were saying, a dog barking at a window. If you have been reading the rest of this book you will know that the model that I work from, is not looking at behavior as a standalone element. It is looking at the conditions under which, the behavior happens. The environment, which prompts that behavior, or cues are the less established points of a road to call it, and the reason why the dog is barking.

Dog will be barking at the window. Okay? So, what happens very often, is the dog is allowed to look, watch, outside the picture window all day long. Somebody walks past, with or without a dog, the dog now starts barking, and the dog stops barking when the person goes away. Now, what is happening from a dog's point of view, is the dog is actually, seeing a number of things.

The big picture window is now the dog's TV, and the dog is now sitting watching that all day long. Just waiting on something happening. Okay? It might be that, that is the only stimulation the dog has during that time. What will then happen, is the behavior of barking is reinforced when the person or the other dog, leaves the dog's sight. So, the dog now starts alarm barking to say, "This is mine. This is my place. Go away." And, the person goes away, and the dog is now immediately reinforced because, the person leaves. The next time what happens, is the dog will bark again, and then the person leaves again. The dog is now reinforced. Okay?

A couple of things, that I generally, will do is very often people will have the settee or the arm chair with the back to the window. The dog now sits on that. Especially, if it is a small dog. Will sit perched on the back of the couch, like this. Watching the whole time. Number of things that you can do immediately to-that is how I explain it to the clients. It is just the dog's television, you know?

What we can do, is we can rearrange the furniture. If that is possible, to make it difficult for the dog. The dog now can't sit there. Okay? We can entertain the dog, who perches on the back of the couch. We can then, move the dog, and ask the dog to get down. Or, physically move the dog. The approach I prefer to do is I ask that-when I see it is a short term thing, is probably, for two or three months, depending on how long this behavior has gone on. You would visually obstruct the bottom of your window.

Now, a lot of people will say, that they will close the blinds or keep the curtains drawn, but then that means that they are not going to let the light into the living room. Which, we don't want.

What I tend to ask them to do, is you would get the translucent window covering, that you can get at the art store, that you would use for your bathroom. Or, just white paper. A roll of white paper from the art store, and tape it along the bottom of your window. Right? Now, what then happens, is that the white paper still allows light into the room. The only aesthetic that it changes is that of the window. The aesthetic changed to your living room is so little, you know? It makes it almost exactly the same amount of light and you can stand up and look out the window. Which, your dog can't do. Usually, the bottom third or the bottom half of the window.

What will happen, is the dog has now no reason to sit on the back of the couch, and watch because, he can't see anything. It is like, putting a screen in front of the television with very little sound. You stop watching that, and you will go away and read a book. Okay? What we can then do, is once we have done that we then, give the dog something else to do. Which, would be enrichment toys. A stuffed big toy, and there is lots of ideas for enrichment. There is a Facebook group called, Beyond the Foodbowl, I think it is.

It has got thousands and thousands of members, and it is about lots of really creative ways to come up with things for your dog to do.

We would start adding in an element of that. The dog has now got something else constructive to do. Other than, eye balling the window. Which, is already covered up, anyway. What I then ask them to do, is after about six weeks or so, is to take out one vertical strip in the middle. Just cut out a vertical strip between one and two centimetres. Take it out, and then tape it again. What will happen then, is even if the dog can see he is getting that tiny movement. It is just a tiny movement. A flicker, and what you may then do, is look, and you can now, mark and reinforce. You can tell the dog he is good because, he has noticed it without barking. Okay?

This now starts allowing you to introduce reinforcement for quiet behavior in the presence of a tiny movement. A week later, you take-you have now got two panels because, we have divided it in two. You take out a vertical strip from your left hand panel, and then a week later a vertical strip from your right hand panel. Another week later, a vertical strip from the panel on the left. Next one, another week on the right. Over the course of the several months, what you are now starting to do is gradually open your window back up again. The whole time you are doing this, you are marking and reinforcing. So, click and treat quiet behavior in the presence of this movement at the window.

With all these things, if we set it up well, we can set and run it up for success as well. We can make it easy for the owner to do it, if they are watching for bad behavior. That would be the first one. The kind of nuisance barking at the window, and I generally, think that is one of the easiest ways to do it because, you are now starting to teach the dog what you want them to do. How you want them to respond. Instead of, stop doing that all the time. You know? We can actually, notice something quiet, and when somebody comes to the door-and I do this with my dog, somebody comes to the door, and he barks, and I say to him, "Thanks, pal." Okay? You have told me somebody has come to the door. I have acknowledged it. So, you now don't need to bark anymore because, you have done your job. You have told me, okay?

When Ian Dunbar – one of my teachers – says when he has this problem-people will say, "My dog barks all the time." Well, really? How strange.

It is a dog.

A dog that barks, you know? Dogs bark. They are going to bark. Just before we come on to the call, I was playing with my dog in the living room, and he was barking and exciting at a couple of things. If a dog was not that, I would start being cautioned by the behaviours, but it is not such a big deal. It is a big deal if, he is barking the whole time, but he is not.

It is the same as if, you were playing football with somebody and they tackle you. You might ha-ha. We have these vocalizations, and I think, it is only reasonable that your dog can have them as well. That would be the first one.

With all these things, it is taking-if you are going to seminars, or you are speaking to other trainers, and it was a trainer who we hosted just a few weeks ago in Glasgow. The first thing I saw Dresher, which I think it was in 2011, she had suggested this covering of the bottom part of the window. She has obviously, heard it from somewhere else. A funny story with that. I used to recommend people buy grease proof paper to do it because; the last time I bought grease strip paper it was like tracing paper.

I then realized, it is now brown. I had said, tape up the bottom of your windows with grease strip paper, and I would drive down the street, and it is actually, as if boarded the house up from inside. This beautiful house, and I was like, "No, let's change that." Yeah, white paper, or something pleasant to look at. Rather than, boarding up your house up. You know? Great for covering your jotters!

It is always look at, what is the reason the dog is barking? Okay, and seeing if we can-I don't know if I explained this the last time. If we think of the behavior as the vehicle, and the reason why the dog is doing it, or the being-whether, it is us or a dog. The reason why they are doing that, what they are trying to achieve by doing that behavior, as the destination. Okay? What we are really looking to do, is examine what destination the dog is trying to get to, and then see, can we put the dog in a different vehicle to do that?

An example of that, is a woman. I had seen her in the park for-only, I think her dog might be three years old, and I spoke to her a few weeks ago. What she does in the morning, is she has got a Cocker-Poo, and she will walk through the park with her friends. Then, they will stop and talk, and what will happen is the dog will run up, drop the ball at her feet, and then bark at her until she picks the ball up with the ball chucker, and throws it. What happens, is that the dog runs forward, throws the ball at her, and then barks. She will then, because the barking bothers her, picks up the ball, and throws the ball for the dog because, that gets her quietness. In order, to carry on her conversation.

I have watched them doing this. If she is engrossed in a conversation, she can actually, start tuning the dog out. The dog will stand there for 30, 40, 50 seconds, and then she picks the ball up, and throws it. What she is actually, teaching the dog to do by doing this, is just keep barking at me because, eventually, I will throw the ball. Okay? I passed her, and I gave her a clicker, and I said to her, "What I want you to do, is when you are talking, and she drops it at your feet, immediately pick up the ball and throw it for her. The next time she comes back, and you see her coming back. Pause your conversation, pick up the ball. See if, you can get two seconds of quiet behavior. Click that, and answer the dog.

What you are now saying to the dog, is rather than barking for these increased periods of time for a ball. Now, be quiet for these increased periods of time, and you will get the ball. Basically, sit politely, and you will get the ball. What we have got there, is the barking, and the quietness are the two different vehicles, and the destination is the chase of the ball. If you are savvy enough about this, you can replace these very, very quickly. The only thing that we don't want to do, is do them both. So, when you start on taking the dog away from one vehicle, you are basically, trying to do everything you can. So that, they don't get back into that vehicle. You know?

I don't know if I have just said this because, I have been thinking in my head, while I was in the back there as well, but it is worth well repeating. The quietness doesn't bother her. Which, is why she doesn't act on the quietness. The barking does bother her.

That is why she acts to the barking.

Looking at our behavior, as well as the dogs, is exactly the same as with the dog barking at the window. The dog will sit there all day long, quietly watching the world go by, and the only time we interact with them is when they are noisy. We really want to be flipping that around. You know?

So to summarise my style and approach, is it is number one having the awareness. First of all, being aware. Open your eyes. Pay attention. Look at what is going on. Number two, take into account the needs of the dog. It is not your trophy. It is not your pet. It is not your companion. Like, a fashion item. It is not a handbag. You know? It is a living, breathing being. Who has needs and wants the same as you do. There is a relationship, number three. There is a relationship going on between you, at any one moment in time. I think, number four, again a recurring theme if you know my work, is there is already an established neurological pathway that, that animal goes down. What you are trying to do is get them to switch to this other track, and go that way instead. You know? Both, get reinforced, or diminished. All the time. It is the same with human beings. It is basic behavioural psychology. It is fascinating. It is exactly the same.

Now let's move onto this first video. Let me tell you about the Beagle.

In fact, I think, this is Alfie. Who, is-I was at school with Angela, when she got in touch with me. A little dog. I think, this is a Cavalier Spaniel. He barks at the television.

We will watch it through. We can watch on it first, and then I will explain everything.

https://www.youtube.com/watch?v=LQuceC9G554

Alfie barks at animals on the television, and that is fairly common as well. I actually, think this has only come to light in probably the last 10 years or so because, with LCD's and plasma televisions, the dog can actually, see that picture clearly. Whereas, with the big tube televisions that we had before, the picture, the dog could not see that as well.

I think, now-there is not a huge amount of research on this, okay? I have spoken to trainers. They would never get the dog reacting to the sound of an animal on television, but certainly not to the sight of them. I think, with the plasma and LCD's, it is as clear as the dog sees it as the dog sees the world. Okay? What Alfie was doing, was anytime an animal would come on, he would just immediately start barking. What we started doing with him, was we put the television on. This was without animals, just people on it, or whatever. Anytime, we glanced at the television while being quiet, we clicked and we treated. We clicked, and we put our treat down.

If you see in the video, the way that I place the treat is also, the way Angela places a treat. She places a treat so that, he turns his back on the television. So that, when he takes the treat he is actually, walking back towards the TV. He gets another shot at looking at it. What I actually teach them, to watch the television quietly, or ignore the television. What I would not like to teach them, not to look at the television. There is a difference. Where we place that treat, sets us up for him coming back, and getting another look at the television again. So, looks at the TV, click, put the treat down. He looks at the TV again, click, put the treat down.

With him because we are talking about that destination of the behavior, the function of the behavior and what he is trying to achieve, it might just be excitement with him. With Alfie and the television, chasing away the animals, being excited because, animals are there because, I can't identify the cause I actually, have to do a different approach. What I am seeing is, I will replace that behavior with another behavior, with another destination. That destination is probably, worthwhile going to anyway. Which, is using this.

If I can treat, I can treat. He sees an animal on the television. I am going to do that method. Until, we see and hear them at the same time on the television for two seconds, while remaining quiet. Then, three seconds, and then four seconds. We should run all that back.

https://www.youtube.com/watch?v=LQuceC9G554

What happens with this is people will now say you are starting to get that little dog a treat for barking. The fact is that the timing of the click isn't as important as the timing of the food. We actually clicked at the right point and then he started barking. The way clicker training works, is the timing of the click has to keep being successful, and doing that is the thing that relevance with the dog. I have spoken with Angela, since this, and she says, that she is now able to watch the TV, and he sits in her lap, and watches. She is not having to use treats so much, anymore. She just sat in the chair, they can watch together without that.

This was all within a space of about 20 minutes. What we will get here is maybe, heading off with the past people whose questions or criticisms about this style of training. At the end of the session like that, would be about 15 and 20 treats. At the start, that might only take a minute. Your training session would only be a minute because, you are having to basically, give him click and treat the second he finishes eating that treat. That is all he can do. As he gets better at that, and you see that in the last set there. He is now, able to look up at the television for three seconds. So, your criteria for reinforcement is now three seconds of quiet behavior while watching television.

Instead of it being, your 20 treats taking a minute. It might take a minute and a half or two minutes, and then your criteria for reinforcement might be five seconds on average. 10 seconds on average, and so on.

Your 20 treats will now, last a longer period of time, and you will now be able to sit and watch an episode of Modern Family, or whatever, over 22 minutes or so that it is on. That might take six, or eight, or 10 treats. Then, you can now start replacing some of those with reinforcements. With other reinforcements. If he looks at the television, and he is quiet? Well done, lad. That is really nice, and then you pet him. You are petting him softly, actually, helps reinforce him more because, what they are trying to do here is match the energy of your reinforcement with the energy of the behavior. If you want settled behavior, you are going to do settled reinforcements. If you want fast behavior, you would fast reinforcements. What we are actually, looking for there, is the reinforcement to be just sit, and relax, and watch television together.

I had another client over the summer, and it was two Westies. It got to the stage where they couldn't have the television on at all, and all we did with that was we just sat with the dog, held her collar, and just petted her softly. Every time she looked at the television, "Settle yourself down. That is lovely, sweetheart. Very nice. Settle down." That nice calmness, settling down. Within a space of two weeks, they got to being able to watch the television again. Very nice.

https://www.youtube.com/watch?v=Zk3g8c9hv34&feature=youtu.be

Okay. This is a wee dog I am working with just now. Saw her last week now, I wish that I had-with this it is always 20-20 hindsight. One or two minutes before this had even started. It is a little miniature Pinscher, and she would go doolally every time the door goes. She will bark all the time. Really sensitive to sudden changes in her environment. You can imagine, you are sitting watching the television. The dog goes suddenly, and up she goes like a rocket. She races down the stairs, and then will bark constantly. I come to the door, a minute or two before I started this video. Chapped the door, and she runs to the door, and starts just barking the whole time. I had my treat bag ready, and I clicked and threw a treat down and she ate it. This worked really well, really quickly.

I said to Caroline, who is the client, "I am just going to go back out. I am going to video this." This is literally the first training session. A dog, who a minute or two before, would be barking the whole time. You will see it here. I don't know if this is me first coming in, or where she opens the door. Yeah, there we go. You hear her barking. Basically, while she is eating that treat, I continue to click, and treat.

Fortunately for this dog, this dog is really food motivated. Basically, clicking so she doesn't get the opportunity to bark. While she is eating, that is quiet behavior, and I can markedly reinforce that.

Really sweet little dog. All of the sudden I'm her best pal. Not surprisingly because I came to the door and fed her. "I like this guy." I saw them again on Monday. That was last Monday. I saw them again last Monday. Really lovely. Really nice dog.

Now I said, dogs really food motivated. Does that mean there are other major motivators that dogs have?

What will happen is all dogs are food motivated. They are alive. Right. If they weren't food motivated then they'd be dead. Other things get in the way of that though.

Very often, what will happen is the dog is so excited and wound up that it just won't take the food at all because, it is so wild, so hyper. Logan my dog, I got him in December. He was so-let's what see if I can find it. Interested and engaged in the outside world. It took him three months, before he calmed down. He was just so wound up. They know what their motion is, and it could be anxiety. It could be excitement. I don't know, and basically, so emotional that he would not take the treats. It took three months of meeting his needs in other ways. He was then, able to walk outside the house, and take him with me. I don't want to say it is not a problem behavior. That is not uncommon. It is uncommon, as for the general dog population, but for problem behavior dogs it is a severe emotional ailment, problem behavior. There is always an emotional behavior, but as I said, near emotional ailment could often be the emotional abuse.

Yeah, its fight or flight – it's not fight or flight or eat.

I will offer the dog food. If the dog takes the food from me, we're all good If the dog doesn't take the food from me, but will take it from their owner, which is generally as it happens to be.

If the dog won't take it at all, then more choices we need to build. We need to build more elements of training with the dog to choose within certain parameters. It's like if I was going to put on a jacket, the question would be do you want to wear your best jacket, or do you want to wear this jacket. It is not "do you want to put your jacket on? No."

Do you want to put your jacket on now, or do you want to put it on when we get in the car?

I don't want to put my jacket on at all. That wasn't on the board.

Introducing an element of choice. This is all the choices that are acceptable to us.

The dog gets to choose.

Again, it is remarkable, and really encouraging to see how quickly the behavior can be amended. That was the first session. I had literally walked in the door. I chapped the door a few minutes before starting recording.

I saw his reaction. I saw how quickly he was reacting to what I was doing. So I told the owner what I was doing. I walked over to Caroline, "I am going to go back out, and video this." I had just arrived two minutes before.

https://youtu.be/UjPKkEhn6Z8

This is Milo, and Milo is a dog who-let's see here. He has multiple motivations for the some of the issues he is having. He is not confident, and he is not social, and they have just had a very-he actually, has got a problem with his back, as well. I think, there is a good chance that he is in pain a lot of the time, as well. The fact that he is not comfortable in his environment, and not social with other dogs, if another dog comes in and at that point, he will then-if the other dog comes in quickly, he has to move quickly. He is going to hurt himself. Which is then compounding the fact that he doesn't like dogs so much.

What we have done with this dog is-of all the three videos that were shown in this chapter, this is the one-it is the same technique that we are using, but we are using it for different reasons. You know? The first two reasons are actually, quite similar, but the third reason we are using the food again to jump start the process, and interrupting a bad behavior. Although, it is nuisance barking, it is a symptom of some other underlying problems that we have got with this dog. He is so reactive, that at a hundred yards away from another dog, he would be pulling at the end of the lead. He would be rearing up, and barking the whole time he saw a dog. Until the dog left, right?

If you go any further away from that, he probably, can't see the dog that well. You know? It is a big distance to be using. Which, means it will then limit some of the approaches that we use because, you can't use some of the stuff that you would ordinarily use, and I did exactly the same thing as well. I started marking and reinforcing. Clicking and treating any kind of behavior that I wanted, or any behavior, which was less than the worst behavior.

I think, I might have mentioned I used this analogy in a previous video. If his worst behavior is level 20 of a 20 story building, I will click level 19 and below. Okay? What will then happen, is over the course of a couple of weeks, 19 now becomes a worst behavior. You will now be levels 18 and below. Then, we just keep chipping away at it. Okay?

What we have done with this little dog, is I actually had to pretty much the same as we have done with Lily, the miniature Pinscher.

People will say that the dog barks the entire time, and yeah they do, but they have to take a breath. If they are taking a breath, it means I can click that. Okay? That might be inhalation.

Any quiet behavior you can get. If your timing is good enough, you can now get in again, and then you can click and treat again. While, they are eating that treat. Okay?

Then, they are still quiet. Again, it is that splitting the path that we talked about there. That is the old behavior, and you are trying to get them at this point here, and then take them on a new road. This is just a minute.

Okay. I do a monthly workshop and we had one last month where-it is a tutorial. It is without your dogs, and people will come, and meet. We basically go through stuff like that. That video there is a minute and 17 seconds long, and we use that as one of our studies. We talked about that for 15, 20 minutes. About all the elements that are going on there okay?

I always think sometimes when I watch some of the videos back, that I could be softer in my approach with the clients, but there is so much happening, and I am trying to train them. Teach them to stay in a boat, while it is happening. To stop it going wrong. Which, is why sometimes I come across as being a little bit sharp, but I explain that to the clients beforehand. If I am barking at you, and barking instructions at you, it is not because I am shouting at you.

You also see there, as well, the amount of skill that, that takes from Pamela there because, she has to listen to me, watch what is going on with the dog, and then try and process and understand it all at the same time. What I do is important because, you can watch this back where I click over, and over, and over again, and then understand it. You are looking at here, and what happens-again, we have certain unrealistic expectations through watching some dogs in the programs on television because, they are well edited, and they are half an hour long.

They are often really heavily based in punishment. Which, means that you can hammer the dog, and get really quick result really quickly. Also, a really-sorry. An end behavior, or lack of end behavior that you like, very quickly. Let's not say that's a good result. It is not good for the dog. What happens there, is that you now sit there, and people will say, "Well, those dogs you see on television can get the dog to be quiet in 20 minutes." I say, "See if I battered you senseless, I could get you to be quiet in 20 minutes, as well." Right? Now I know I'm being flippant about this but its not that he is battering a dog senseless, but he is really heavy handed with them. You see this in TV shows.

BUT he is building resentment from there on. It is going to pop back out later on, okay. Or, it will just be so suppressed that the dog will just shut down, and not do anything. Which means, when you are trying to train them to do stuff, they won't do it because, they won't want to do anything.

Just like humans. You batter them, and they will shut down. You know?

You see a couple times in the video, he moves towards that dog, and starts barking, and she just calls him back in. Tries to get some quiet behavior, and then marks him, and watches, and then there is a better-the next point that we watch this, there is a time there where he looks at her, and barks. We mark and reinforce that. The intensity of the bark is low. He is not barking at her. He is looking at her and barking. He is barking because, there are dogs in the environment, and that is what he does when there are dogs in the environment.

We can get rid of the barking later on, okay? That is horrible on that dog though. That dog is being-one of the most enjoyable, successful cases I have had this year because, he was so extreme when I started.

Again, with that dog, that was in the first session, and that session there was three weeks, I think. You know? But Pamela, every time she goes out the door. She has got a clicker. She has got a bag of treats. She is watching the environment. We can get-it is not that positive training is as quick, it is that as a society we are not as skilled in doing this stuff, as we are with punishment.

We've been brought up in punishment. Our parents, our teachers, our church, whatever. Society is-we got a penal system. It is big crime and punishment. Everything is about hammering unwanted behavior. Which, means that we are not skilled and then what happens, and you will know this for yourself when you start paying people compliments they think "What's your game?"

We are just not used to receiving compliments.

We are not used to receiving positive reinforcement because, we are just not skilled at it. It is not that this treatment is slower. It is just that we are not as good at it, as we are with punishment. We will watch it one more time.

Another thing – Where I told her to give the dog treats to his mouth. As opposed to, putting them down. What was the distinction about?

What happened the first time, when we are doing this-it is an interesting point, and it came up during the tutorial as well. The first treat she delivers, to his mouth. Sorry, she throws the treat out. Okay? It is knowing when to-if we accept that all behavior modification is about manipulation of the environment, and manipulating environs so that behaviours that we want can happen, and then us manipulating what reinforcement we can use. So that, we can manipulate future behavior. The whole thing is about manipulation.

We can just park that. Let's accept that, that is what is going on. Cos it is, right?   That is a different video.

When I place the-I think, we covered this in one of the other webinars. Where I place the reinforcement, sets up the dog to do the next behavior.

If I am working with the dog in a public park, and I click. He comes towards me, and I click, and I toss the treat 10 or 15 feet away, he goes out to get that treat and he now has available behaviours. Okay?

He has a wider range of available behaviours to do next, than if I click and give the treat to his nose. What he has now got, is he has got a much narrower spectrum of available behaviours.

What happened the first time, was he was doing well. She clicks, and she puts the treat out, and I have noticed something in him. I said to feed them to his nose now because, what I want him to do is I want him to be successful. I would rather him be successful doing one behavior. Which, is the only one he can really do in that instance. Rather than, give him the option of doing five behaviours and getting it wrong. This dog is not skilled enough yet to discern which one he should be doing. As he gets better at that, I can now start broadening out the range of choice that he has. The skill in this, or the art form, whatever you want to call it, is knowing when to remove choice, and when to give choice to your learner. Like this here, if we were broadcasting this live, we are removing lots of choice from the learners that are watching this. If they are watching it, and it is pre-recorded, they can now pause this, go to the toilet, go make a cup of tea, and watch it later on. They are not missing out.

Depending on what you are doing, how you set up your environment for your learner, dictates how successful you are going to be. What we did there, was we started feeding them to his mouth, and as we are walking away, and coming back, she said, "His mouth got to the ground." I can't remember. I think I actually, said, "You can put it on the ground because, we are walking away at that point, and with this dog he will follow us. He won't go back, and bark at another dog. You are actually, setting him up again to be successful."

What we have done there, is we made it easier for Milo to see the dogs by Pamela's positioning. She is facing the dogs. He is now having to turn over his back to see where they are, and I don't want that. I want him going, "There is a dog. Who cares?" I don't want him saying the dog is not there, the dog is not there. It is me and you. It is me and you. We actually, want him doing, "Yes, a dog."

Will she turn her back to them, or will she leave the door open for him to see beyond there. You know? Again, the intention being aware. You have to be in up time. You have to be out. Externally focused. Not in your head thinking about the work, or thinking about what you are having for tea tonight. You are there to help the dog.

We see there he is on a long line there, but you can see there I am not holding him there. There is a big loop in that line. He has got about 15 feet of slack that he can move about, and he is choosing to stand next to her. When he makes that choice, we reinforce it, without manipulating him. We are manipulating him in a way that is kind for him. Rather than, a way that is harsh.

Okay. Dogs barking and it is driving you nuts? Those are some of the interventions that you can do.

Yeah, it is not difficult. Again, I make it look easy. Yeah, it is things you can do on your own, and obviously, if you need my help, I am available to do that. Usually, I can get people an appointment within seven to 10 days.

Now we know every dog is different, but I will ask the difficult question. How quickly can we see a result with a nuisance doggy barking?

You saw there with Milo. Milo, is one of the most-I don't want to say extreme. That is not the right word. It is not kind. The most intense dogs I have had. His behavior has been the worst, if you like. You know what I am thinking of. The most, you know? That took three weeks of work. Two or three weeks of work.

Yeah, and then I had them again on Monday there. He had made another significant change again. It was lovely. What we are looking to do there, we will cover the aggression one in another chapter. We are working to get to a stage where we are not having to work. The environment becomes reinforcing in itself. We are not having to do-it is not top heavy with our intervention. The dog just becomes settled enough in the environment, that oh, cool. Yeah, I can do this.

We can do it another way.

I can confidently say to somebody, that you could be seeing results a month from today. Or, a month from the part where they start working with me

With Milo-again, Milo is an extreme case. With Milo, we saw results within a space of an hour. Within the space of an hour I can show the client significant change. I say to them, "This is within an hour. Where are you going to be in two weeks' time, if you keep doing this? In two months' time? In six months' time?" If I went to the gym, and my coach was immediately saying to me, "I can get you benching 100 kilos today." Not a problem, but if a trainer said to me, "You're going to have to keep coming back if you want it. Keep lifting like that." We can get very good results really, really quickly. It is just whether they last or not. Depends on that depth of reinforcement history.

And if you love your dog, care about your doggy, then why wouldn't you?

Again if you want to get in contact with me the website is best. www.Glasgowdogtrainer.co.uk. There is an email from on my website, and that is the best way to get to me. My email is enfil@glasgowdogtrainer.co.uk. Also, my Facebook, as well, and there was some videos on Facebook. Lots of content on my YouTube channel, and I have also got a WordPress. Which, all of those are available through my website. The buttons are all on the homepage now too, but I updated them all.

As ever it is all about the welfare of the animal, and having a nice relationship with your doggy. That is what it is all about. I say he or she doesn't have a choice. He is your slave. He can either be your welcome guest, or he can be your slave.

CHAPTER FIVE – DOG NOT COMING WHEN CALLED

The topic I'm going to talk about in this chapter accounts for about one third of my working time with clients. In about one third of all the appointments that I have there will be some element of the dog not coming back when called. So this chapter is all about recall - getting your dog to come back to you when you ask it to. This comes up in my one to one client work and also in the seminars that I speak at all over the world and I've been doing this for eight years at the time of writing this book.

The topic comes up whenever the client lets their dog off the lead at the park – the dog run up towards other dogs, towards other people or taking off chasing squirrels and rabbits. The dog owner is then left shouting and screaming in the background. So when they come to me it's a matter of going through the process with them and explaining to them that they have to have something that the dog wants.

Conventional dog training says you have to be more interesting than everything else that that's going on in the environment. I think that that's an impossible task – if you are in a Beagle the owner is not going to be more interesting if the Beagle wants to go hunting for rabbits, but you can teach the Beagle that access to the hunt will come through me, we will do the hunting together but we will only do it at a specific time and your dog can learn that. People will come to me and ask me how do we get the dog to come back when I call it back and then we resolve it and it's basically building more of a relationship between you and your dog with greater reinforcement between you and your dog so the dog wants to come back to you as a fun person to be with so either good things happen when I come back to mum or dad, play happens, big belly rubs happen or access to other cool things in the environment happens. So if the dog wants to go and see another dog, call them back first and then take them to see the other dog or person so all the cool things, all the good things that the dogs like to see in the environment are accessed through us so we become the gatekeeper.

So I've got another video lined up for you:

https://youtu.be/JLo85Dn2hmo

So this is Debbie and Rocky and all are doing is asking Debbie to reinforce any engagement. So if you watch it again you'll see a couple approaching with a cocker spaniel so we slow down and stop. Rocky checked in with us and then we reinforce good behaviour with a little bit of food. So these are the foundations, the basic parts to get the dog to the park. If you spend a little bit of time when you take the dog to the park get your dog to engage with you and then move closer towards other things in the environment, we used to call them distractions - things that would distract your dog's attention away from you, such as other dogs, footballs, bikes, scooters - all that kind of thing that the dog will find interesting so whenever the dog reengages with you, you reinforce that.

If you get this foundation in place at the start it will reap massive rewards later on – what most people do is they take the dog out, let the dog off the lead and give it free access to people, dogs, all the cool stuff and wonder why they can't get the dog back – because the only time they call the dog back is at the end of the walk when I wanna put it back on the lead and go home. So the dog has learned that, and now there is no incentive for the dog to come back to you.

So in the video your see the couple with the other dog approaching so I deliberately got the client to bring the dog to a halt and sit down and pay more attention to the client that the other dog. In fact the dog offered to sit - the sit was actually unimportant. Rocky likes to sit because the previous owner reinforced it quite a lot so he offered that but the sitting part is not necessary. What I'm looking for is for the dog to engage with you while the other dog is coming and we start off really easy so if we play the next video in the same session…

https://youtu.be/PeHGvz0fT6M

Now what's interesting in this video is that Rocky started to lag behind a little bit and moved away from Debbie and all Debbie does is she holds him on the lead as if to tell him "What you've just come from has past now" so it's actually restricting him a little bit so we do the same again in terms of someone approaching so you can see here he becomes interested in something on the ground and Debbie continues to walk. All she is doing with the lead is preventing him from moving any further back and then he comes back up and walks back with her.

So the other dog became the distraction so it's a case of immediately asking for your dog's attention and reward the dog with something to eat so that's more important. You're conditioning this over a number of repetitions. Now notice I say that we ask for the dog's attention we don't get the dogs attention. The way that we teach is that there is a cooperative approach between you and your dog so that sometimes you absolutely will get your dog's attention but what we want to do is have the dog willingly offer his attention.

Now as a general rule your dog will have a poor recall. Another dog in the same environment is a signal for your dog to go and play with the other dog and the dog is and reinforced when it goes and plays with the dog and has a good time. So when we use a long line right now in the early stages of training what we say to the dog is "There is a dog over there but I'm going to prevent you from going to see, BUT if you check in with me I will play with you and I will do something good." Now over a number of repetitions the other dog then becomes a signal for your dog to check in with you and you can reward it with a variety of things whether it's food or play.

Only then do you say to the dog okay it's okay to go and play with them. So the dog checked in with you and effectively asked for permission so when you say 'yes on you go pal' then you can go and play.

Now your recall signal can be anything that the dog perceives – it could be a smell, a sound. Shouting your dog's name, ask him to come can be recall. Clapping your hands can be a recall cue. Search and rescue dogs finding a person who is buried in the snow. They will have a signal that is the signal for the dog to run back and tell the handler that there's someone in the snow. This thing in the environment can be a signal for any behaviour; you just need to train that.

So we see in the video with Rocky he checks and sees the dog, checks in with the owner and what we did at the start with him was we just allowed him to look at the dog from a distance and when he turned around and checked in then we then reinforce that. If you do that multiple times which means dozens of times. In fact dozens and dozens - they don't take a long time to do. In a 40 minute walk he could see 40 other dogs anyway. If you're doing that three or four times a week at the end of the week you've had dozens and dozens of repetitions anyway so if you get good practice and that you can install it quite quickly. So the real problem is when dog owners give their dogs unrestrained access to other dogs and people when out on walks from an early age so you end up fighting up against that early conditioning the dog has already learned that all this other stuff that is really, really cool and we are boring and you wanna flip that on its head and see the other stuff is boring, I'm where the really good stuff happens.

So in the next video we're going to get a little bit more advanced with Rocky.

https://youtu.be/WcMxuCZrBxI

So you see Debbie walking towards Lynsey who is holding a bag of treats. I'm just using the treats as an example – this is just to set this up. Debbie walks away but you see how Rocky engages with her all the time. Debbie looks over shoulder and invites him in so he comes back towards this, your mark it with a click and then we take it back. Take Rocky back and give him his treat. Let me do the same again. Debbie doesn't have any food or toys with her here but what she is teaching Rocky is "Come with me and the good things happen."

So to summarise what you just saw there - Debbie is the dog owner and she doesn't have any food or toys on her at that moment. Lindsey who used to work with us she has the treats. This is about Rocky leaving something cool to go with mum he doesn't have anything cool okay?

So we can then practice this and then transfer it into other situations so Lindsey is holding a bag of treats, Rocky comes up and looks up at her but doesn't get any. Debbie walks away, calls him in, he comes back to her telling him he's a good lad and then gets taken back to Lynsey with the treats and give him the treat that you just left. Rocky learns that he has to do something good in order to get something good so the importance is gradually shifting from one thing to another. I know we can substitute Lindsey for another dog or a person – you can basically say to Rocky you don't need to bother about that - come to me and the good stuff will happen here. It may not happen immediately, or within a few seconds and I'll take you back to meet that person so it gets Rocky checking in all the time with mum and asking 'okay what are we doing?' It gets him looking in the right direction. And because he's a big chunk of a dog – he must be about 70 or 80 pounds or something and you can see that's been done with him on a slightly loose lead. The lead is just there, it's used as a barrier effectively and it means the dog can't run off with nothing to stop them but that's getting a little bit of structure.

Take a look at this next video all the way through and then we will go back and go over.

https://youtu.be/qS1v5rNMUPY

So in this video the owner is the blonde woman. She's got a young dog, she moves towards him, she moves towards the right hand side of the screen and there's people walking up the path there. So she walks far enough then starts to slow down. Now very often if you have some sort of semblance of connection with them they will be aware when you stop. She slows down and stops. That then encourages her dog to slow down and stop. The dog does the same then checks in with her and only then did she throw the ball for him in the opposite direction from the people, and he then runs and gets that ball. So what that dog likes to do is he likes to run around and chase things. I'm giving him the opportunity to chase something in the presence of something that is not to be chased. Which is other people and other dogs. So if you watch that video again

What I do is I look at the science of behaviour change and how you can apply it well. So the owner walks forward slows down and stops… pauses… and then she throws the ball. She gives him the opportunity to chase something. That's what he likes to do.

With Rocky he likes to spend time with mum and eat food, so we use that as a reinforcement. You see in the future video that the dog likes to play tug so that's what we use in that case. So each case is based on the same thing as the antecedent, the cue of what's going on in the environment, the people, dogs, smells, then he checks in with me and the consequence is I get something good which is going to make the recall much easier next time.

So the training is formulaic but the application of it is where your experience and your art form comes into it. And then it's all about judging that individual relationship between dog owner and dog. The motivation can change in a heartbeat – the dog might be happy to take the food from you when there are no other dogs around but as soon as another dog appears they may prefer to run and chase something so it's all about knowing what reinforcer to use that what time.

So we are utilising the dogs existing preferences in the first place so if it wants to run and chase things then you want to incorporate that into your intervention and what we also want to do is build in some kind of robustness into the dog to teach that he will not always be able to chase things whenever he likes.

So with my little dog all of the recall training was based around 'see another dog chase the ball, see another dog chase the ball'. There were also other times when we were walking with her on a lead to the park or along the street and if you saw another dog she couldn't chase that dog soyou then say to her that. No you can't do that right now.

https://youtu.be/G47lcOoVaZA

So in the next video you will see that a few more other dogs come into the scene and we give her access so she can play with other dogs but at the right time she is disengaging and that's when we recall her and throw the ball. Prior to the session she would not have been able to leave the dogs alone, she would just continuously want to play but because we made mum and dad interesting and engaging and fun to be with, and we didn't stop her from playing with the other dogs, we said you can go and look at the other dogs and go and say hi – it's now your choice, and she made a good choice there and chose to have more engagement with us. So within the space of 40 odd minutes we got a dog who would see other dogs and make a beeline for them to disengaging from other dogs and coming back to us.

You can see how doing the right things and applying the science well very quickly we get a result. You see the dog run out to the other animals, she quickly says hi and then she disengages and comes back to the owner. The dog is happy because it's getting everything it wants.

What I'm also doing is I'm teaching the client to watch their dog, and look out for the signals of the dog reengaging in with them. Because very often the dog will check in with us and we wanna be on top of that and be ready, but what happens is people will look at their dog or look at the other dogs while all this is going on. We want them to pay attention purely on their own dog. If you want your dog to pay attention to you, you need to pay attention to your dog.

If you're staring at your phone you're missing the queues. That happened just this morning in the park I was working with a big dog, super friendly American bulldog, big and boisterous and bouncy and this German Shepherd came charging in from nowhere and when I looked up the guy was tapping away at his phone with his dog 100 yards away from him and he was completely oblivious. That's not safe actually. It's not safe to not know where your dog is. The connection is broken because you're not paying attention.

https://youtu.be/mlF7Ih5r5_k

In this next video you see the dog goes and says hi to another dog. Ideally we should have the dog on a harness but we're using a long line – you should have your dog in a harness. He says hi to the wee dog, and you'll see it's exactly what we did with Rocky and the other dogs and the other videos as well. He says hi again to the dog and we let him and I wind in the lead a little bit just to prevent him from leaving. Then he makes a choice there so we give a little bit more distance from the dog and had a look, and then he tries to take off with the dog but I prevent him from doing that – that's the thing that you have to teach the puppy from an early age that he can't have everything that you want all the time. And it builds resilience in them. In this case that puppy is only 15 weeks old and if people did that from the get go with the puppies you would have much better recall, but what happens if people take the dogs out and in the name of socialising the dog they give the dog unfettered access to other dogs and people and what their effectively doing there is they're building a massive learning in the dogs saying that other dogs and people are the fun experience that you're seeking.

The dogs at least we give them enough freedom and good experiences around other dogs and people so they're not frightened of them, but I think you would have a much better life with the dogs if you taught the dog that the good stuff is gonna come through us and if you're going to make a decision that your dog is going to play with other dogs on a regular basis, you need to recall train them and that means restricting the access. Our little dog Watson was given unrestrained access for the first year of her life and had several other dogs in her life and as such was a total nightmare because she couldn't see another dog and control herself – it was just "Oh My God there is another dog and it's time to play" so then she got massively frustrated that she wasn't being allowed to see the other dogs.

What then happens at that point with some owners is the dog starts whingeing and barking and the owner starts correcting them and they go from being a friendly frustrated dog to being a dog that's potentially frightened of other dogs because it knows the owner is going to give a hard time every time a dog appears. Take your dog out to the park and play with them - don't take your dog out to the park and let them play with other dogs if you want your dog coming back to you. Take them out and play with them over and over again and play with him for a little while then let them go for a sniff. Let them have a look at another dog and then bringing back food and play with some reward then do cool stuff with him - just hang out with them. The more you do that the more the dog will want to come back towards you.

Recall is actually one of my favourite things to train – it's also stupidly easy if you look at it in the right way. Prevent the dog from doing things that but you don't want doing, and reinforce the things you do want him doing. Not this, that. It's simple when you see it like that but I think it's really beneficial to let you see step-by-step what actually happens and you're setting a precedent at a very early age…so you need to get it right . Just like with children, dogs are just like little furry people.

https://youtu.be/qN9D4bAM56k
.
In the last video in this chapter we have a young Staffordshire cross and she is super interested in other dogs. She comes in to say hi, we stop there on the lead, she comes back in and then she gets to play with the tug toy. There are several times which comes back to re-engage with the owner with mum rather than going to see the other dog. We let them have a look again and then reward with another tug. Now I'm not holding the dog on a lead there, she is making the decision herself. If she makes the wrong decision we will prevent her from running off but I'm not on her back the whole time – but having had as much choice as we can she starts to learn "Oh it's this one" it's not "This is the only one we can do". But effectively setting up the dog to make the decision that we want her to make and then reinforcing it.

Every time she makes the wrong decision we then have access to reinforcement for that decision. Which is as she did there, she pulled towards a dog and we said no you can't do that, but we said it without shouting at her or correcting her harshly or tugging on the lead or telling her NO you cannot do that one and that was all done relatively kindly. There is nothing aggressive or forceful or resistant and all the stuff that we've seen. There are a couple of times we absolutely are stopping the dog from moving off i.e. physically stopping the dog, but the difference between a Steward standing preventing you from getting access to a pub and manhandling you down the stairs – there is a huge difference to the way that we can prevent behaviour happening. We can do it relatively gently.

If you look at police officers at football grounds, all that is, is a physical prevention to stop the fans from getting each other that there is nothing violent about that, there is nothing particularly forceful in it. It changes behaviour because it teaches them - you can't do that one. That's the way I look at it and the better your lead handling skills the kinder it is on your dog.

The key is cooperation – it's a synergistic relationship, it's about attentiveness, it's about paying attention to your dog. In that last video it was all about letting the dog stare and look at other distractions and then it gets to decide when it reengages with the owner. The dog gets to decide when it comes back to you and then gradually realises that coming back to you is the best place to be.

Now there are going to be sometimes when you need to step in and intervene. If she had been staring too long at the dog coming in I might help her out by calling her name, or smacking my lips or rustling a bag of treats or something like that so I can certainly try and help her out. But if it's not safe at that point - for example the other dog might be showing body language that's aggressive and unfriendly or whatever, I will physically move that dog because I'm not going to put that dog in a position where it's going to be harmed or it's going to make a serious training or behaviour mistake.

We are not letting the dog do whatever she wants whenever she wants it – there are rules to this but were saying these are the rules I'm going to help you understand what they are and then you can make that choice and I'll make it worth your while. She then starts to want to make that choice and if she is reinforced well 90 percent of the time from us for re-engaging us with us while in the presence of other dogs and she's only reinforced 10 percent the time to play with the other dogs under the same circumstances the dog will come back to us 90 percent of the time.

You want to fill your dog's behavioural repertoire with good stuff. So with my big boy dog, everything we do together is 'you and me pal, me and you are out here together to have fun and we're not interested in speaking to people I'm interested in coming out here and spending time with you.' And as a result of that he wants to spend time with me.

The other thing as well and you can see in the video with Debbie and Rocky - if you stand still the dog will tend to stand still. If we walk towards the dog, the dog will tend to walk away from you. If you walk away from your dog your dog will tend to come with you, so what happens is people see their dog start to trot towards other dogs and will then chase them. What we are effectively doing is backing them up but if you shout 'come on let's go' and run in the opposite direction then the dog is much more likely to go "Oh cool we're going that way" and come with you.

But what tends to happen is that people stand still and shout at their dog without moving their bodies. We need to move our bodies, we need to move our feet. These are all subtle distinctions but now that you've read them they're going to strike you as DING! That's obvious. It's a system, it's a formula, its step by step, anyone can learn it and anyone can apply it. There are certain rules to the game but like everything else in life, if you know the rules then you can play it. This is just about understanding how behaviour is built and the more you understand how behaviour is built, the better you will be at building those behaviours that you desire.

The final question that often comes up is "When do we get the dog off the long line?" What I say to clients is "When was the last time you had to physically use that line to stop your dog from leaving? Or when did you last have to physically go and get your dog? If your answer is "Oh it's been weeks and weeks" then that's the time to consider – that under those circumstances – now is probably the time to start taking the line off. And remember that it's not an "All or nothing" thing – you can always put the line back on for more training. I've done this with one of my own dogs – if it's relatively quiet I'll let her off the lead to run around. If there are other dogs nearby then I'll put her back on the lead, or let her trail it, and with this training I have successfully recalled that dog from chasing other dogs and from chasing deer or foxes.

So it is possible and it's possible without using an electric collar which a lot of people think is not possible but it is. We have been conditioning recall in dogs for hundreds of years – people have been hunting with their dogs or herding with their dogs for centuries and they've gotten great recall and all of that is done off lead. But this is the easiest way that I've found. If people don't use the long line then at the same time as us trying to build a history of the dog coming back to us, the dog is continuing to build a history which is already there of going to seek out and meet other dogs, so both of these conflicting desires are increasing at the same time which is not ideal. We want the new behaviour level increasing so that it gradually overtakes the old behaviour. So this is the easiest way I've found to add it in and it works – it works if you do it. I know it works because I have done it so many times and I've done it with my own dogs.

CONTINUE YOUR DOG TRAINING

"I have never met a dog I couldn't help, however I have met humans who weren't willing to change"

Cesar Millan

Stop Putting Up With An Aggressive Dog Barking Inappropriately…

"Here's How You Can Quickly and Easily Apply Advanced Dog Training Methods Guaranteed To Turn Your Dog Into An Obedient Happy Friend… Without Aversion Techniques!"

Dear Friend,

How much is a happy, healthy dog worth to you and your family?

Suppose you could just click a mouse and get expert tips from an experienced Dog Trainer & Behavioural Consultant.

Imagine… your dog behaves itself, comes when you call and walks beside you like a champ.

Sounds too good to be true?   Well, it isn't if you have the right know how.

Think about it. An experienced Dog Trainer is the most powerful asset you could ever hire for your dog's welfare. A compassionate Trainer who trains dogs well but still gets the changes that you'd love to see is worth their weight in gold.

But Finding That Assistance Is The Hard Part… It could take you years and can cost you a small fortune to figure out just the right combinations that make some Dog Training work – while others fall flat on their face.

But instead of knocking yourself out trying to search for just the right person you can now have it at the touch of a button inside a new online course called:

"John's School"

At last! The answers to the top 5 most frequently asked questions are here.

Which Of These Powerful Modules Could You Use To Have A Well behaved Obedient Dog?

Nuisance barking

- Discussion on dealing with nuisance barking

Not coming back when called

- Discussion on what recall is and how to improve it

Pulling on the lead/leash

- Discussion on how to improve your dog walking next to you, without pulling

Does you dog jump up on you?

- Discussion on teaching your dog to keep 4 paws on the floor

Dealing with aggressive behaviour

- Discussion on dealing with aggressive behaviour

Okay, So What's The Cost For This Incredible Resource?

I currently charge a minimum of £75 per hour for one to one training.   So at bare bones minimum you're getting hundreds of pounds worth of quality dog training at your disposal.

But I'm not going to charge you anywhere near that amount or even my minimum consulting price. In fact, your total investment for all five modules is only $35

Look at it this way -- $35 is really a painless drop in the bucket compared to the time and money you're going to waste on ineffective books, DVD's and YouTube videos this year. That's why…

You Really Can't Afford Not To Invest In This Training!

It's easy to get started right away. Just click below:

https://johns-school-2cfd.thinkific.com/courses/5-top-problems-5-solutions

Get ready to change your, and your dog's lives forever.

Sincerely,

John McGuigan

P.S. Just think! You'll never again suffer through the pain and hassle of nuisance barking, not coming when called or aggressive behaviour.   Check it out now!

Printed in Great Britain
by Amazon

83832555R00037